SCHOLASTIC

ZANY MISCELLANY

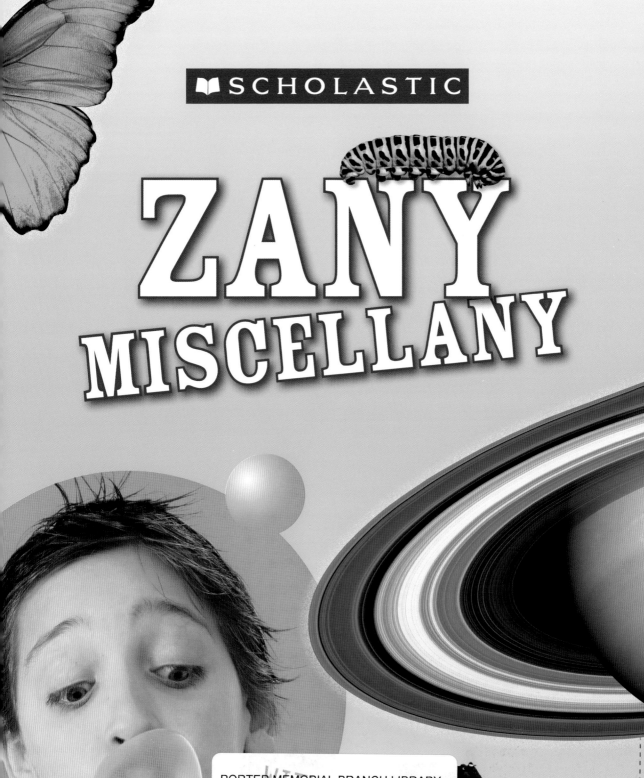

SCHOLASTIC

ZANY MISCELLANY

pulsar

A spinning star that sends out pulses, or beams, of radiation.

Nerd Word

NERD WORD

Can't understand what the brainy scientists are talking about? Help is here! Let our nerd explain the word.

STAT-O-SPHERE

A Stat-O-Sphere is a bubble filled with loads of information.

What IS a ZANY MISCELLANY?

WELCOME TO ZANY MISCELLANY, an encyclopedia with a big difference—it's the world's first muddle-o-pedia!

Each page contains a mind-boggling array of stats, facts, and stories. You don't need to look anything up—just choose a page and see what you discover. Who knows what you will find out! Where does hair get its color from? What's the best ship for pirates? What's the difference between a meteor and meteorite? Who was the first computer programmer? And why were the first roller coasters called "Russian hills"? Want to know these things and a whole lot more? Then dive in!

FACTOID

A jewel beetle can smell wood smoke from 50 miles (80 km) away.

W–O–R–M–H–O–L–E

Check out:
Dolly
Page 54

WORMHOLE

Wormholes are shortcuts that connect sections that have something in common. Why not take a ride through some Wormholes and see where you end up?

What is the most dangerous type of shark?

Page 6

?

Have you been paying attention? Inside each question mark is a question about something on another page. And if you see a question you want to know the answer to, you'll be able to find out for yourself.

FACTOID

Just because something is strange doesn't mean it isn't true. That's exactly what Factoids are—facts you've never thought of knowing.

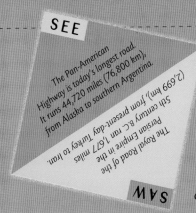

SEE

The Pan-American Highway is today's longest road. It runs 44,720 miles (76,800 km), from Alaska to southern Argentina.

The Royal Road of the Persian Empire in the 5th century B.C. ran 1,677 miles (2,699 km), from present-day Turkey to Iran.

SEESAW

They say history repeats itself—but not always! The SeeSaw feature gives examples of how times have changed over the years.

FACTPILE

When you stack some related facts, you get a Factpile. On its own each fact is interesting; pile them up and you get the complete picture about everything from dinosaurs to the White House.

FACTPILE / ROCKETS

A rocket is powered by burning fuel that is directed through a small hole, or nozzle.

Rocket fuel does not need air to burn, so it can work in space.

The first rockets were fireworks made in China in the tenth century.

The largest rocket ever used was the Saturn V. It could carry the weight of 12 trucks into orbit.

VENN TEN

Even things that are very different can be connected, and a Venn Ten will show you how. Did you know that nine of the world's top ten sunniest places are not among the top ten driest? Or that one of the least polluted countries in the world is also one of the largest users of nuclear energy?

VeNN TeN

MOST VISITED COUNTRIES
France * United States of America * Spain * Italy * United Kingdom * China * Mexico * Poland * Canada

Austria

Bolivia * Mongolia * Ethiopia * Serbia * Niger * Chad * Mali * Belarus * Afghanistan
LANDLOCKED COUNTRIES

WANTED

Jack the Ripper (1888)

Birthplace: Unknown
Job: Unknown
Crimes: In 1888, several women were found murdered in London. The police named the unknown killer Jack the Ripper because of the violent way he killed. Jack might have had as many as 11 victims, but was never caught.

REWARD

WANTED

Read about some of history's bad apples in our mini Wanted posters.

PeOPLe-OPOLY

Thomas Crapper (1836–1910)

Thomas Crapper was an English plumber who sold toilets in the 19th century. He did not invent toilets that flushed, but he was the first person to sell them to ordinary people. Beforehand, only a few wealthy homes had flush toilets. Despite his link with the toilet, historians think his name is not linked to the slang words for going to the bathroom.

PEOPLE-OPOLY

What are the most complicated things in the universe? People. Each one of us is different, and here are some stories about a few people who made their marks in unusual ways.

GOOF-A-THON

Dead Sea Scrolls

In 1947, a shepherd boy was searching for a lost goat in the hills of Qumran, beside the Dead Sea in what is now Israel. The boy came across a cave that contained jars filled with papers. The papers became known as the Dead Sea Scrolls. Experts think the scrolls were written before the time of Christ, but they contain similar teachings. Some believe the scrolls were the work of a religious group that might have inspired Christ.

FLOP TEN

Things don't always go right. Sometimes they go really wrong! A Flop Ten is a Top Ten with a difference—a list of the biggest mistakes, accidents, or naughty tricks, ever.

GOOF-A-THON

Some of the greatest inventions were accidents—cornflakes, superglue, and nonstick skillets. Goof-a-thons tell the stories of how some simple goofs had happy endings.

Carnivorous Plants

Common Name: Venus flytrap **Scientific Name:** *Dionaea muscipula* **Method:** Uses a spring trap. Hairs inside the leaves make them snap shut, trapping the insect, which decomposes and is digested.

Common Name: Pitcher plant **Scientific Name:** *Darlingtonia californica* **Method:** Has a bulbous chamber, which fills with water. Insects slide down into it and drown.

Common Name: Butterwort **Scientific Name:** *Pinguicula vulgaris* **Method:** Traps insects on its sticky surface. The leaves curl over it and digest it.

VeNN TeN

Top 10 ENDANGERED SPECIES

Black rhino * Giant panda *
Beluga sturgeon * Goldenseal *
Alligator snapping turtle *
Hawksbill turtle * Bigleaf mahogany *
Green-cheeked parrot * Mako shark

Bengal tiger

Great white shark * Bull shark *
Hammerhead shark * Lion *
Cougar * Grizzly bear *
Reticulated python *
Alligator * Crocodile

Top 10 MAN-EATERS

W – O – R – M – H – O – L – E

Check out:
John Venn
Page 16

TEN MOST DANGEROUS SHARKS

Species	Unprovoked attacks	People killed since 1580
Great white	323	75
Tiger	131	29
Bull	99	22
Sand tiger	70	2
Requiem	48	8
Nurse	47	0
Blacktip	40	1
Hammerhead	32	1
Blue	32	4
Shortfin mako	25	2

radioactivity

The radiation, including alpha particles, nucleons, electrons, and gamma rays, given off by a radioactive substance.

Nerd Word

Space Missions to Planets

Launch	Mission	Event
1962	Mariner 2 (USA)	First to return data on Venus
1964	Mariner 4 (USA)	Sent the first pictures of Mars
1970	Venera 7 (USSR)	First landing on Venus
1972	Pioneer 10 (USA)	First flyby of Jupiter
1973	Pioneer 11 (USA)	First flyby of Saturn
1973	Mariner 10 (USA)	First flyby of Mercury
1975	Viking 1 and 2 (USA)	First landing on Mars
1977	Voyager 2 (USA)	First flyby of Uranus and Neptune
1989	Magellan (USA)	First detailed map of Venus
1989	Galileo (USA)	First Jupiter orbiter and probe
1996	Mars Pathfinder (USA)	First Mars exploration by rover
1997	Cassini (USA/Europe)	First Saturn orbiter/Titan probe
2004	Messenger (USA)	First Mercury orbiter

ICE AGE MaMMaLS

Wool and fat kept these mammals warm during the ice age. (The last ice age ended 9,000–15,000 years ago.) They became extinct 11,000 years ago as the world warmed up.

Mammoth	Woolly Rhinoceros	Cave Lion
Scientific Name: **Mammuthus**	Scientific Name: **Coelodonta**	Scientific Name: **Panthera leo**
Order: **Proboscidea**	Order: **Perissodactyla**	Order: **Carnivora**
Size: **10 ft. (3 m)**	Size: **13 ft. (4 m)**	Size: **11½ ft. (3.5 m)**
Cave Bear	**Giant Ground Sloth**	**Saber-Toothed Tiger**
Scientific Name: **Ursus spelaeus**	Scientific Name: **Megatherium**	Scientific Name: **Smilodon**
Order: **Carnivora**	Order: **Pilosa**	Order: **Carnivora**
Size: **10 ft. (3 m)**	Size: **20 ft. (6 m)**	Size: **4½ ft. (1.4 m)**

THE LEANING TOWER OF PISA

The Leaning Tower was built between 1173 and 1360 in Pisa, Italy. Some historians thought that the strange tilt of the building was created intentionally, but it is now believed that the tilt was really created by accident.

Kittens

When kittens are first born they are blind and helpless. However, after only 4 weeks these furry bundles will become lively little copies of their parents. By the time kittens reach 8 weeks old, they like to play, and at 12 weeks old, they are ready to leave their mother and find a new family to live with.

GOOF-A-THON

Play-Doh

Noah and Joseph McVicker were trying to invent a new type of wallpaper cleaner in 1956 when they accidentally stumbled on the recipe for Play-Doh. They realized that it would make a great substitute for children's modeling clay because it is easy to shape and not toxic. Since then, over two billion cans have been sold. The first Play-Doh available was off-white.

FACTOID

The great shortstop Cal Ripken, Jr. played a staggering 2,632 games in a row, breaking Lou Gehrig's record for the most consecutive games played.

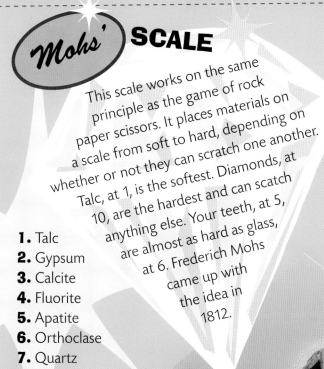

Mohs' SCALE

This scale works on the same principle as the game of rock paper scissors. It places materials on a scale from soft to hard, depending on whether or not they can scratch one another. Talc, at 1, is the softest. Diamonds, at 10, are the hardest and can scatch anything else. Your teeth, at 5, are almost as hard as glass, at 6. Frederich Mohs came up with the idea in 1812.

1. Talc
2. Gypsum
3. Calcite
4. Fluorite
5. Apatite
6. Orthoclase
7. Quartz
8. Topaz
9. Corundum
10. Diamond

SEE

George W. Bush was elected president in 2000 and again in 2004. His father, George H. W. Bush, had been president from 1989–93.

John Adams was president from 1797–1801. His son, John Quincy Adams, became president in 1825 and served one term.

SAW

When did **Hawaii** become a **state?**

Page
16

SPHINX

Paws: 50 ft. (15 m) long
Head: 30 ft. (9 m) long
Body: 150 ft. (45 m) long
Ordered by: Khafre
Age: 4,636 years old

HOW to SURVIVE an AVALANCHE

PeOPLe-OPOLY

Joseph Ignace Guillotin
(1738–1814)

This French doctor was against the death penalty, so he decided to make executions swift and painless. The blade of the guillotine, which is named after him, was designed to cut off the victim's head quickly and cleanly.

Being able to breathe is the key to survival, so drop anything you are holding and immediately cover your mouth and nose with your hands. Before the avalanche stops, use your hands to create an air space in front of your mouth and nose, then start digging your way out before the snow hardens around you.

W–O–R–M–H–O–L–E

Check out:
Saint Bernard
Page 20

LEOPARD SPOTS

CHEETAH SPOTS

JAGUAR SPOTS

parapsychology

The study of strange things, such as ghosts and telepathy.

Nerd Word

DINOSAURS IN THE MESOZOIC ERA

FACTFILE

Cretaceous Period
(145–65 million years ago)

Last of dinosaurs—duck bills, tyrannosaurs, and horned dinosaurs

Jurassic Period
(213–145 million years ago)

Early heyday of dinosaurs—first birds evolve

Triassic Period
(251–213 million years ago)

First dinosaurs and archosaurs—meaning "ruling lizards"—appear

FACTOID

The planet Saturn is so light it would float in water if you could find an ocean big enough.

VeNN TeN

Top 10 GIRL DOG NAMES

Princess * Lady * Sandy *
Sheba * Ginger * Brandy *
Daisy * Missy * Misty

Samantha

Emily * Emma *
Madison * Abigail *
Olivia * Isabella *
Hannah * Ava * Ashley

Top 10 GIRL NAMES

Where in the **body** can you find the **tibia**?

Page **21**

The DIFFERENCE between an AFRICAN . . .

Height: 11 ft. (3.3 m) at shoulder
Weight: 7½ tons (6.8 tonnes)
Ears: Big ears
Back: Concave curve
Trunk: Two bumps at end

The tomato is a fruit, not a vegetable.

W – O – R – M – H – O – L – E

Check out:
La Tomatina
Page 50

The Microwave Oven

In 1945, Dr. Percy Spencer was testing a new vacuum tube called a magnetron when he discovered that the chocolate bar in his pocket had melted. Intrigued, he tried another experiment. This time he placed some popcorn kernels near the tube and watched as the popcorn popped all over his lab. The first commercial microwave oven went on sale a year later.

... and an INDIAN MALE ELEPHANT

Height: 10½ ft. (3.2 m) at shoulder

Weight: 6 tons (5.4 tonnes)

Ears: Smaller ears

Back: Humped

Trunk: One bump at end

The Statue of Liberty was a joint effort between France and the United States, with France building the statue and the United States the pedestal. The statue, made of 100 tons of copper and 125 tons of steel, was shipped in 350 pieces aboard a French vessel, the *Isere*. It was erected on the pedestal, the country's largest concrete structure in 1886.

FACTOID

The world's largest robot arm measures over 250 ft. (76 m) and is used to clean jet airliners.

Town and Country	Pluto Nash	Cutthroat Island	A Sound of Thunder	The Alamo	Monkeybone
Lost $95m	Lost $93m	Lost $82m	Lost $74m	Lost $69m	Lost $65m

10 most expensive movie flops

Stat-O-Sphere

cartilage

The gristle that covers the ends of bones to prevent them from rubbing against one another.

Nerd Word

World's Largest Deserts

Desert	Location	Area
Sahara	Northern Africa	3,500,000 sq. miles (9,000,000 sq km)
Arabian	Southwestern Asia	1,000,000 sq. miles (2,600,000 sq km)
Australian*	Australia	576,000 sq. miles (1,491,800 sq km)
Gobi	Central Asia	500,000 sq. miles (1,300,000 sq km)
Patagonian	Argentina	260,000 sq. miles (673,000 sq km)
Kalahari	Southern Africa	190,000 sq. miles (490,000 sq km)
Taklimakan	China	123,550 sq. miles (320,000 sq km)

*This is a series of deserts.

The GREAT Pyramid of Khufu

Built:
c. 2500 B.C.

Height:
481 ft. (147 m)

Base Length:
756 ft. (230 m)

Base Area:
13 acres (5.3 ha)

Weight:
5.75 million tons (5.2 million tonnes)

Number of blocks used:
2.3 million

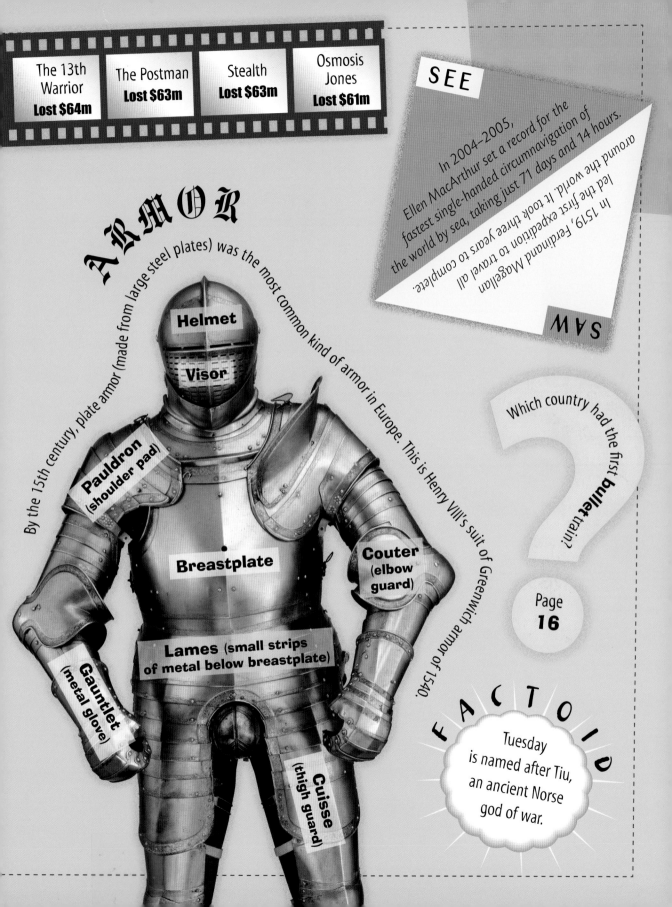

SEE

In 2004–2005, Ellen MacArthur set a record for the fastest single-handed circumnavigation of the world by sea, taking just 71 days and 14 hours.

In 1519, Ferdinand Magellan led the first expedition to travel all around the world. It took three years to complete.

SAW

ARMOR

By the 15th century, plate armor (made from large steel plates) was the most common kind of armor in Europe. This is Henry VIII's suit of Greenwich armor of 1540.

- Helmet
- Visor
- Pauldron (shoulder pad)
- Breastplate
- Couter (elbow guard)
- Lames (small strips of metal below breastplate)
- Gauntlet (metal glove)
- Cuisse (thigh guard)

Which country had the first **bullet train**?

Page **16**

FACTOID

Tuesday is named after Tiu, an ancient Norse god of war.

PeOPLe-OPOLY

John Venn
(1834–1923)

British logician and philosopher, who is famous for inventing Venn diagrams, which are used in many fields, including set theory, probability, logic, statistics, and computer science.

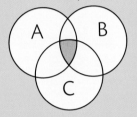

Venn diagrams show all the possible mathematical or logical relationships between different groups of things (sets).

Poisonous Spiders

Spiders inject poison into their victims by biting them with special fangs called chelicerae. Although all spiders hunt this way, only a handful have poison powerful enough to kill people.

FACTFILE

THE RoCK CYCLE

Hot liquid magma cools to form solid igneous rock.

Igneous rock can be rough or smooth.

Some igneous rocks: rhyolite, basalt, pumice, kimberlite, gabbro, granite, syenite.

Rocks are eroded by glaciers, wind, and water and carried into rivers and seas.

Lighter rock particles collect in rivers, lakes, and seas, forming sediment.

Sedimentary rock forms when layers of sediment are compressed and cemented together.

Some sedimentary rocks: limestone, chalk, sandstone, breccia.

THE BULLET TRAIN, JAPAN

The Japanese bullet train, or shinkansen, was the world's first high-speed train. Nowadays, it regularly runs at speeds of over 185 mph (300 km/h).

SEE SAW

The United States has had 50 states since Hawaii became a state in 1959.

In 1787, Delaware became the first "state." By 1790, 13 states had signed the U.S. Constitution.

THE SUN

Age: 4.6 billion years old **Star type:** Yellow main sequence star **Diameter:** 870,000 miles (1,400,000 km) **Core Temperature:** 27,000,000°F (15,000,000°C) **Key Fact:** Hydrogen in its core is changed by nuclear fusion, making it hot

GOOF-A-THON

Post-it Notes

While working on the chemical formulae for stronger glues, Spencer Silver, a researcher for the 3M office-equipment company, accidentally discovered a superweak glue. It was dismissed as useless, until a colleague, Arthur Fry, thought of applying strips of it to paper.

FACTOID

The first in-flight hot meals were served in 1927, 13 years after the first powered flight.

The largest invertebrate (an animal without a spine) is the colossal squid, thought to be more than 40 feet (12 m) long.

coprolite

This is a polite word for fossilized dinosaur poo. Yuck!

Nerd Word

R I C H T E R SCALE

If you want to know how powerful an earthquake is, you need to know the Richter scale. It measures how much energy is released by an earthquake based on readings recorded by seismographs.

Magnitude	What happens	How often?
Less than 3.0	You won't even feel it	1,000 per day
3.0–3.9	Makes things vibrate a little	49,000 per year
4.0–4.9	Shakes things but doesn't break them	6,200 per year
5.0–5.9	Damages some buildings	800 per year
6.0–6.9	Damages buildings in an area about 60 miles (100 km) across	120 per year
7.0–7.9	Can cause serious damage over large areas	About 18 per year
8.0–8.9	Can cause serious damage over areas hundreds of miles across	About one a year
9.0 or greater	Causes devastation over several thousand miles	About one every 20 years

W - O - R - M - H - O - L - E

Check out:
Mohs' Scale
Page 9

SEVEN VENOMOUS CREATURES

WHAT
Black widow spider
Blue-ringed octopus
Box jellyfish
Funnel-web spider
Inland Taipan snake
Marbled cone snail
Stonefish

WHERE
Worldwide
Pacific Ocean
Pacific and Indian oceans
Australia
Australia
Pacific and Indian oceans
Pacific and Indian oceans

W–O–R–M–H–O–L–E

Check out:
Man-Eaters
Page 6

VeNN TeN

LARGEST Cities
São Paulo * Mumbai *
Shanghai * Kolkata *
Delhi * Buenos Aires *

Tokyo * Mexico City *
New York * Los Angeles

Chicago * Paris *
London *
Osaka/Kobe *
Philadelphia *
Washington, D.C.

RICHEST Cities *

*Based on GDP (gross domestic product)—how many goods and services were produced—in 2005.

Like all trees, trees grown as Christmas trees take in carbon dioxide from the air and give out oxygen. While they are growing, an acre of Christmas trees makes enough oxygen for 18 people every day. In seven years, a Christmas tree will be big enough to sell. For every Christmas tree sold, three new trees are planted so there will be more next year.

FLOP TEN

Baseball's Longest Losing Streaks

Philadelphia Phillies
23 GAMES
1961

Baltimore Orioles
21 GAMES
1988

Boston Red Sox
20 GAMES
1906

Philadelphia Athletics
20 GAMES/1916

Kansas City Royals
19 GAMES
2005

Philadelphia Athletics
18 GAMES/1920

Philadelphia Athletics
20 GAMES/1943

Detroit Tigers
19 GAMES
1975

Washington Senators
18 GAMES/1948

Washington Senators
18 GAMES/1959

SEE

Number of people who have climbed Everest before 2003: 1,655, with more than 30 climbers known to have reached the peak on the same day.

Number of people who climbed Everest in 1953: Two (Sir Edmund Hillary and sherpa Tenzing Norgay).

SAW

Saint Bernard

This breed of giant dogs got its name because it was bred to rescue travelers who got into trouble on the St. Bernard pass in the Swiss Alps. These dogs are big enough to drag a man, and they have thick, furry coats, so they don't get cold in the snow and ice.

W-O-R-M-H-O-L-E

Check out:
Avalanches
Page 10

BIRTHSTONES

- January — Garnet
- February — Amethyst
- March — Aquamarine or Bloodstone
- April — Diamond or Rock Crystal
- May — Emerald or Chrysoprase
- June — Pearl or Moonstone
- July — Ruby or Carnelian
- August — Peridot or Sardonyx
- September — Sapphire or Lapis Lazuli
- October — Opal or Tourmaline
- November — Topaz or Citrine
- December — Turquoise

HUMAN SKELETON

- Skull
- Mandible (jawbone)
- Humerus (upper arm)
- Clavicle (collar-bone)
- Sternum (breastbone)
- Spine (backbone)
- Pelvis
- Rib cage
- Coccyx (tailbone)
- Ulna
- Radius
- Metacarpals
- Patella (kneecap)
- Femur (thighbone)
- Fibula
- Tibia (shinbone)
- Metatarsals

GOOF-A-THON

Safety Glass

French scientist Edouard Benedictus discovered safety glass in 1903 after he knocked a bottle of laboratory chemicals off a shelf. The glass didn't shatter and he realized that the cellulose nitrate within the bottle had coated the inside and prevented it from breaking.

The letters on the first typewriters were placed alphabetically. However, typists typed too fast and the keys got stuck together. The modern "QWERTY" keyboard was invented to stop keys from sticking together by keeping commonly used letters apart. It also slows down typists.

FACTOID

A human head weighs an average of 9½ pounds (4.25 kg).

Stat-O-Sphere

10 Deadliest Earthquakes Since 1900

Date	Epicenter	Magnitude	Deaths
1976	Tangshan, China	7.8	650,000
2004	Sumatra	9.1	280,000
1920	Gansu, China	7.8	200,000
1927	Tsinghai, China	7.9	200,000
1923	Tokyo, Japan	7.9	143,000
1948	Turkmenistan (formerly part of the Soviet Union)	7.3	110,000
1908	Messina, Italy	7.2	100,000
2005	Kashmir/Pakistan	7.6	80,000
1932	Gansu, China	7.6	70,000
1935	Quetta, Pakistan	7.5	60,000

WANTED

Billy the Kid
(1859–1881)

Name: William H. Bonney
Also known as: William Antrim, Henry McCarty
Birthplace: New York City
Job: Cowboy
Crimes: Killed 20 men
Jail escapes: Four
Death: Shot by Pat Garrett on July 14, 1881

REWARD

entropy

The tendency of the universe toward chaos, randomness, and disorder.

Nerd Word

Chameleons can change their color completely in less than two minutes from a basic yellow.

Quick Camouflage
Chameleons can't turn just any color, only the yellows, browns, and greens of leaves. To match the pattern and color of the leaves they are standing on, chameleons shrink or enlarge colored cells in their skin.

The 2008 Olympics in Beijing, China, will have more than 10,500 competitors.

The first modern Olympics took place in 1896 and had only 241 competitors.

SAW

Harry Potter

Address:
#4 Privet Drive,
Little Whinging, Surrey

Owl:
Hedwig

Parents:
Lily and James Potter

Birthday:
July 31

Quidditch position:
Seeker

I ♥ THE BROOKLYN BRIDGE

One of the first suspension bridges to be built, New York's Brooklyn Bridge is 6,016 feet. (1,834 m) long and joins Manhattan and Brooklyn. It was built between 1870 and 1883 and approximately 27 workers died building it. Soon after it opened, rumors spread that it was going to collapse. In the rush to escape, 12 people were killed.

FALSE TEETH

George Washington's were made of teeth from horses and donkeys set into ivory.

The Etruscans, an ancient Italian civilization, made the first false teeth in the seventh century B.C.

About 25 percent of adults over 60 no longer have their own teeth.

How does a **streetcar** travel?

Page
93

FACTOID

Thanksgiving was made a national holiday in 1863 by Abraham Lincoln.

FLOP TEN

10 stupid criminals

The bank robber who gave his real name and address to the bank worker.

The thief who got trapped inside the bank and had to call the police for help.

The thieves who stole police-tracking devices, which led the police to their hideout.

The thief who stole a bank's camera, which recorded him doing it.

The robber who fainted when he realized there was no money at the bank.

The robber who gave up because his homemade mask did not have any eyeholes in it.

The raiders who left their truck's bumper and license plate chained to a cash machine.

The woman who was jailed after asking Guns For Hire, a team of Wild West circus performers, to shoot her husband.

The thief who left his own $20 bill on the counter as he ran off with $15 from the cash register.

The robber who told a store he would be back in 30 minutes to hold up the place. The police were ready when he came back.

GOOF-A-THON

Bubble Gum

Walter Diemer was an accountant at the Fleer Chewing Gum Company. After a day at the office, Walter liked to make his own gum at home, trying out new ingredients. In 1928, Walter made a gum mixture like no other. It was less sticky than chewing gum, and much stretchier. Walter found that he could blow the gum into bubbles and soon convinced his bosses to sell his accidental invention as Dubble Bubble.

chlorophyll

The green chemical in leaves that turns sunlight into sugar.

Nerd Word

FACTOID

Shining a light on the back of the knees makes people feel more awake. No one knows why.

STONE HENGE

Stonehenge is a 3,500-year-old structure in England. It was made from 82 huge slabs of stone, which weighed up to 4 tons (3.6 tonnes) each. Each pillar was dragged from the Welsh mountains, 245 miles (395 km) away. On Midsummer Day (June 24), the sun rises in line with Stonehenge's main entrance. No one is sure what Stonehenge was used for, but it was probably a sacred place.

FACTFILE

GLOBAL WARMING

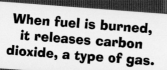

When fuel is burned, it releases carbon dioxide, a type of gas.

The sun's energy passes through the carbon dioxide and warms the ground.

However, the carbon dioxide blocks heat from the ground from going back into space.

The planet gets gradually warmer, climate patterns change, and weather becomes more extreme.

Stat-O-Sphere

10 Longest Rivers

River	Continent	Length in miles (km)	Mouth
Nile	Africa	4,157 (6,690)	Mediterranean Sea
Amazon	South America	3,968 (6,387)	Atlantic Ocean
Mississippi	North America	3,896 (6,270)	Gulf of Mexico
Yangtze	Asia	3,859 (6,211)	East China Sea
Yenisei	Asia	3,449 (5,550)	Arctic Ocean
Ob-Irtysh	Asia	3,362 (5,410)	Arctic Ocean
Yellow	Asia	2,900 (4,667)	Yellow Sea
Congo	Africa	2,716 (4,371)	Atlantic Ocean
Amur	Asia	2,714 (4,368)	Pacific Ocean
Lena	Asia	2,647 (4,260)	Arctic Ocean

Where would you find a **pauldron?**

Page 15

Louis Braille
(1809–1852)

Frenchman Louis Braille invented a writing system for blind people. The system is called braille after its inventor. It uses patterns of raised dots for each letter, which the reader feels with his fingertips. Braille got the idea for his writing from a system used by soldiers to communicate at night.

A cow cannot bite grass. Instead, it curls its tongue around the grass and rips it out of the ground.

FACTOID

It is so hot on Venus that a lead pipe would melt.

THE SAME BUT DIFFERENT

Although some twins are identical, others are nonidentical. Identical twins have the same genes. They are always the same sex and look very similar. Nonidentical twins have different genes and can be different sexes. They are born at the same time but are no more closely related to each other than normal brothers or sisters.

COUNTRIES WITH HIGHEST BIRTHRATES
Mali * Chad * Uganda * Somalia *
Angola * Liberia * Dem. Rep. of Congo *
Marshall Islands * Sierra Leone

Niger

Burkina Faso * Afghanistan *
Sierra Leone * Gambia *
Guinea-Bissau * Senegal * Benin *
Ethiopia * Mauritania

COUNTRIES WITH FEWEST READERS AND WRITERS

torque

A force that causes an object to spin around.

Nerd Word

INCA TRAIL

The Inca trail is a path that runs about
53 miles (85 km) through the Andes
Mountains to the ruins of Machu Picchu in
Peru. Every year, 180,000 tourists walk the
trail. It takes about four days to reach
the amazing Incan city, which is located
at the top of a steep mountain.

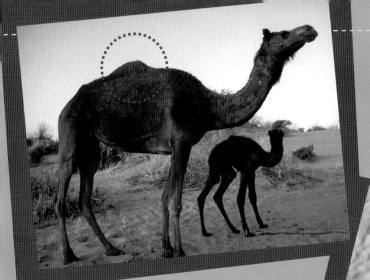

ONE HUMP OR TWO?

Not all camels are the same. Dromedaries have just one hump (above) and are more common. They live in North Africa, the Middle East, and they have even been shipped to Australia. Bactrian camels have two humps (right). They live in the cold deserts of Central Asia.

WANTED

Vlad the Impaler
(1431–1476)

Name: Vlad Dracula
Birthplace: Romania
Job: Tyrant
Crimes: As a cruel ruler of Romania, Vlad had many people put to death. Most of them were impaled—a sharp stick was stuck through their bodies. (Vlad was the inspiration for the famous vampire story, *Dracula.*)

REWARD

W–O–R–M–H–O–L–E

Check out:
Drinking Blood
Page 52

What is the world's largest **invertebrate**?

Page
18

SEE

The fastest car ever built is ThrustSSC. It is powered by two jet engines and can drive at 763 miles (1,228 km) per hour–faster than sound!

The world's first car, made in 1885 by Karl Benz, had three wheels and a top speed of 9 miles (15 km) per hour.

SAW

Smilodon

The scientific name for the saber-toothed tiger, which is extinct.

Nerd Word

A "BANANA" kick starts straight, then curves.

Where are the **pillars** of **Stonehenge** from?

Page
27

BENDING IT

A top soccer player can make the ball swerve in the air to fool another player. He makes the ball spin as he kicks it, and the spin causes the ball to move sideways in the air like a wing makes an airplane rise upward.

LASERS

A laser is a beam that contains just one wavelength, or color, of light. Lasers were invented in 1960. Today, they are used in many ways. A laser reads the information on a DVD, CD, or barcode. Surgeons use lasers to burn away cancer, and lasers are bounced off the moon to measure how much Earth's land shifts each year.

FACTOID

Astronomers have found stars made from pure diamond.

HOW FOSSILS FORM

The remains of a living thing, such as a shell or bone, become buried in damp mud.

The damp stops these remains from rotting away.

Water trickling through the ground coats the remains in minerals, so they become as hard as stone.

The mud is squeezed for millions of years. It becomes solid rock, which protects the fossil until it is exposed.

FACTFILE

Where is **Machu Picchu?**

Page **30**

Penicillin

In 1921, Alexander Fleming, a Scottish scientist, began studying a bacteria that caused nasty infections. He grew the bacteria in little dishes. One day Fleming noticed that one of his dishes had become moldy, and the bacteria was not growing around the mold. He realized that the mold, a fungus called *Penicillium,* was killing the bacteria. By chance, Fleming had discovered the first antibiotic—a medicine that kills bacteria.

Two masts

Pirate Ship

The perfect pirate ship is fast and easy to steer. Many pirate crews terrorized the seas in a sloop. This fast ship was small enough to hide in shallow water, out of reach of big warships. However, the ship all pirate captains wanted to capture was a brigantine. This was also fast, but it had a big hold for storing plenty of treasure and was built to fight far from land.

Long bow for high-speed sailing

Room for 100 men

HOLIDAYS IN THE DESERT

The United Arab Emirates is a small country in the deserts of the Middle East. It grew rich by selling oil, but now its leaders—the sheikhs—want their country to be a holiday destination. Although there aren't many beaches, that's no problem. The superrich sheikhs have built brand-new islands in the sea to make room for the hotels.

FACTOID

Chihuahua dogs are named after a state in northeast Mexico. They were first bred 1,000 years ago.

The smallest dogs in the world!

SEE

Modern chemists have identified about 90 elements in nature. They have even manufactured new ones in laboratories.

SAW

The ancient Greeks thought things were made from a mixture of four elements: earth, water, air, and fire.

TUTANKHAMEN

King Tutankhamen was the pharaoh of Egypt 3,330 years ago. He reigned only for a few years but is remembered today for the fabulous death mask discovered in his tomb. The mask is made of 22 pounds (10 kg) of gold and decorated with jewels. The blue stripes are made from lapis lazuli imported from Afghanistan.

FACTOID

Lions were kept in the Tower of London until 1835.

World's LONGEST Suspension Bridges

Bridge	Country	Length	Completed
1. Akashi Kaikyo Bridge	Japan	6,529 ft. (1,990 m)	1998
2. Great Belt Bridge	Denmark	5,328 ft. (1,624 m)	1998
3. Runyang Bridge	China	4,888 ft. (1,490 m)	2005
4. Humber Bridge	United Kingdom	4,626 ft. (1,410 m)	1981
5. Jiangyin Suspension Bridge	China	4,544 ft. (1,385 m)	1999
6. Tsing Ma Bridge	Hong Kong	4,518 ft. (1,377 m)	1997
7. Verrazano-Narrows Bridge	United States	4,258 ft. (1,298 m)	1964
8. Golden Gate Bridge	United States	4,260 ft. (1,280 m)	1937
9. High Coast Bridge	Sweden	3,970 ft. (1,210 m)	1998
10. Mackinac Bridge	United States	3,800 ft. (1,158 m)	1957

MOST ACTIVE VOLCANO: Mount Etna in Sicily has been erupting almost continuously for the last 3,500 years.

LARGEST ERUPTION: Two million years ago, a giant crater was formed in Yellowstone, Wyoming, when an explosion threw 600 cubic miles (2,500 cu km) of rock into the air.

LARGEST VOLCANO: Mauna Loa covers more than half of the island of Hawaii. It rises to 2½ miles (4 km) above sea level. It also plunges down 3 miles (5 km) to the seafloor.

PeOPLe-OPOLY

Thomas Crapper
(1836–1910)

Thomas Crapper was an English plumber who sold toilets in the 19th century. He did not invent toilets that flushed, but he was the first person to sell them to ordinary people. Beforehand, only a few wealthy homes had flush toilets. Despite his link with the toilet, historians think his name is not linked to the slang words for going to the bathroom.

neutrino

A tiny particle that is released when two atoms fuse together.

Nerd Word

WHITE-KNUCKLE RIDES

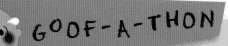
FACTOID

President Franklin Roosevelt moved Thanksgiving a week earlier so people could do more Christmas shopping.

The first roller coasters were sled runs built through steep hills in Russia. In 1804, the first roller coaster track—known as a Russian Mountain—was built in Paris. The world's highest and fastest roller coaster is Kingda Ka in New Jersey. It is 456 feet (139 m) high and the cars travel up to 128 miles per hour (206 km/h). Enthusiasts travel the world to ride on the best roller coasters. The fastest rides are after a thunderstorm, when the rails are warm and wet.

See the SEA COWS

In the distant past, seafarers mistook manatees and dugongs for mermaids. However, these strange mammals, which are also called sea cows, are distant relatives of elephants. Sea cows live in warm seas. They graze on sea grass growing in shallow waters.

Stat-O-Sphere

10 Most Spoken Languages

Language	No. of Speakers	No. of Countries
Mandarin Chinese	1.12 billion	11
English	480 million	40
Spanish	332 million	34
Arabic	235 million	14
Bengali	189 million	3
Hindi	182 million	5
Russian	180 million	16
Portuguese	170 million	8
Japanese	125 million	3
German	98 million	16

Are You My "MUMMY"?

The ancient Egyptians preserved the bodies of kings as mummies. But they did not stop there. Cats, crocodiles, baboons, and many other animals were also mummified. The Egyptians believed the animals were gods.

THE WHITE HOUSE

The White House was officially known as the Executive Mansion for the first 90 years of its existence.

John Adams was the first president to live in the White House. In 1800, he moved into the building while it was still being built.

The White House is made from gray sandstone, which is easily damaged by rain. The stone is protected by a covering of white lime. That is why the White House is white.

Most of the White House had to be rebuilt between 1948 and 1952.

FACTOID
The word "mugger" comes from the Sanskrit word for "crocodile."

WORLD CUP WINNERS

Brazil	**5 wins**
Italy	**4 wins**
Germany	**3 wins**
Argentina	**2 wins**
Uruguay	**2 wins**
France	**1 win**
England	**1 win**

SEE SAW

A modern airliner can carry more than 500 people from England to Australia in fewer than 23 hours.

In 1938, it took nine days to fly from London, England, to Sydney, Australia. Up to 15 passengers traveled in luxurious "flying boats."

10 RARE MAMMALS

Animal	Country	How many left
Vancouver Island marmot	Canada	29
Sheath-tailed bat	Seychelles	50
Javan rhino	Indonesia	60
Hispid hare	India	110
Northern hairy-nosed wombat	Australia	13
Iberian lynx	Spain	120
Dwarf water buffalo	Philippines	200
Malabar large-spotted civet	India	250
Ethiopian wolf	Ethiopia	442
Bactrian camel	Asia	950

Giant Cactus

The Sonoran Desert in North America is home to the mighty saguaro cactus, which takes decades to grow. Eventually, it can grow 50 feet (15 m) high, but in its first ten years it grows only ¾ inch (2 cm) tall. After that the growth speeds up, but the cactus won't flower for another 50 years.

What is the most dangerous type of shark?

Page
6

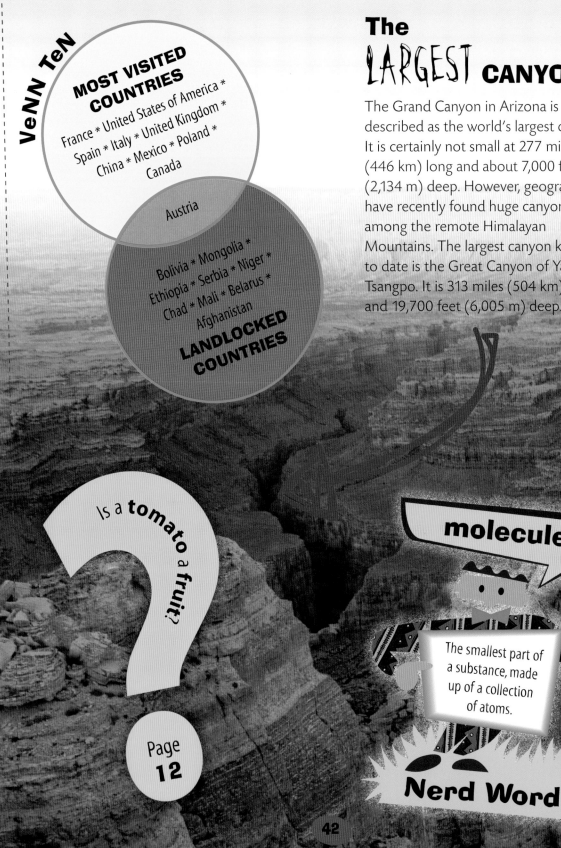

VeNN TeN

MOST VISITED COUNTRIES

France * United States of America *
Spain * Italy * United Kingdom *
China * Mexico * Poland *
Canada

Austria

Bolivia * Mongolia *
Ethiopia * Serbia * Niger *
Chad * Mali * Belarus *
Afghanistan

LANDLOCKED COUNTRIES

The LARGEST CANYON?

The Grand Canyon in Arizona is often described as the world's largest canyon. It is certainly not small at 277 miles (446 km) long and about 7,000 feet (2,134 m) deep. However, geographers have recently found huge canyons among the remote Himalayan Mountains. The largest canyon known to date is the Great Canyon of Yarlung Tsangpo. It is 313 miles (504 km) long and 19,700 feet (6,005 m) deep.

Is a **tomato** a **fruit?**

Page
12

molecule

The smallest part of a substance, made up of a collection of atoms.

Nerd Word

STINKING GIANT

The world's largest flower belongs to the titan arum of Sumatra. The spadix, the fleshy center part of the bloom, grows to 10 feet (3 m) tall. The flower has a scent that smells like rotten meat.

Dead Sea Scrolls

In 1947, a shepherd boy was searching for a lost goat in the hills of Qumran, beside the Dead Sea in what is now Israel. The boy came across a cave that contained jars filled with papers. The papers became known as the Dead Sea Scrolls. Experts think the scrolls were written before the time of Christ, but they contain similar teachings. Some believe the scrolls were the work of a religious group that might have inspired Christ.

A TITANIC TRAGEDY

The Titanic was supposed to be unsinkable. However, on the liner's first voyage in 1912, an iceberg ripped a hole along one-third of its hull. The ship sank in two and a half hours. More than 1,500 people drowned.

Liger

The liger is a giant cat that has a lion for a father and a tiger for a mother. Lions and tigers never meet in the wild, so ligers are born only in zoos. A liger looks similar to both its parents, with a mane and faint stripes. However, it is generally larger than the wild cats. The child of a male tiger and female lion is called a tigon.

What's the BILL?

Toucans live in the forests of South America. The toucan's large bill, or beak, is used to crack nuts. The bill has toothlike ridges for gripping food.

WANTED

Jack the Ripper
(1888)

Birthplace: Unknown
Job: Unknown
Crimes: In 1888, several women were found murdered in London. The police named the unknown killer Jack the Ripper because of the violent way he killed. Jack might have had as many as 11 victims, but was never caught.

REWARD

Walking on the Moon

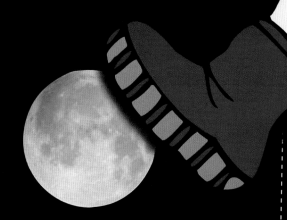

Only 12 people have walked on the moon. American astronauts traveled to the moon as part of the Apollo Program between 1969 and 1972. The first astronauts to set foot on the moon—Neil Armstrong and Buzz Aldrin—never went more than 110 yards (100 m) from their spacecraft. Later crews were less cautious. Some even played golf. Apollo 15 took a car to the moon in 1971, and the crew stayed for nearly three days.

London's BURNING

The Great Fire of London destroyed central London in 1666. A fire started in a bakery in Pudding Lane, near London Bridge. The wind spread the flames quickly. After four days, 13,000 buildings had burned down, including St. Paul's Cathedral. The fire was stopped when a wide gap between the crowded houses was created to stop the flames from spreading. Luckily, only a handful of people were killed.

PeOPLe-OPOLY

Albert Einstein
(1879–1955)

Although he is the most famous scientist in the world, most people do not understand Albert Einstein's discoveries. Einstein came up with the theory of relativity, which explains how space, time, and matter (the stuff inside all things) are related to one another. The theory explains how matter can be turned into energy using the famous formula $E = mc^2$.

Throwing STONES

In curling, teams slide large stones toward a target, or "house," on an ice rink. The stones naturally curve, or "curl," off course. Players steer a stone by brushing the ice. Brushing melts the ice, so the stone keeps moving in a straight line.

F A C T O I D

Nearly twice as many men as women live in Qatar.

SAMURAI

The samurai were the knights of Japan. They were expert horsemen and fought with steel swords. A samurai followed a code called Bushido, the "way of the warrior." Under the code, samurai lived a simple life and were very loyal to their commanders. If he broke the code or was defeated in battle, a samurai was expected to commit suicide.

What is the Mohs' Scale?

Page
9

46

FACTFILE

Sea HORSES

Sea horses are fish that live in warm, shallow seas.

They curl their tails around seaweed to avoid being washed away by the tide.

The fathers are unique in the animal kingdom because they give birth to the young.

Sea horses are now very rare because so many have been caught for use in Chinese medicines.

Stat-O-Sphere

10 Largest Empires in History

Name	Size	Ruler	Year*
British	14.1 million sq. miles (36.5 million sq km)	King George V	1921
Mongol	12.8 million sq. miles (33.2 million sq km)	Kublai Khan	1279
Soviet	10 million sq. miles (25.9 million sq km)	Leonid Brezhnev	1989
Spanish	7.3 million sq. miles (19 million sq km)	King Charles III	1759
Arab	5.1 million sq. miles (13.2 million sq km)	Caliph Al-Walid	715
Qing (Ching)	4.6 million sq. miles (12 million sq km)	Qianlong emperor	1899
French	4.3 million sq. miles (11.1 million sq km)	President Albert Lebrun	1938
Portuguese	4 million sq. miles (10.4 million sq km)	King Henrique	1580
American	3.9 million sq. miles (10.1 million sq km)	President Theodore Roosevelt	1908
Persian	2.9 million sq. miles (7.5 million sq km)	Darius the Great	486 B.C.

*This is the year when the empire was at its peak.

HOOVER Dam

The Hoover Dam is a huge slab of concrete across the Colorado River in Arizona. More than 100 people died making the dam. The dam uses the water running through it to make electricity, which is supplied to the nearby city of Las Vegas.

10 largest bankruptcies

WorldCom, Inc.
$104 billion
July 2002

Enron Corp.
$63 billion
Dec. 2001

Conseco, Inc.
$61 billion
Dec. 2002

Texaco, Inc.
$36 billion
April 1987

Financial
Corp. of America
$34 billion
Sept. 1988

Refco, Inc.
$33 billion
Oct. 2005

Global
Crossing Ltd.
$30 billion
Jan. 2002

Pacific Gas
and Electric Co.
$29 billion
April 2001

Calpine Corp.
$27 billion
Dec. 2001

UAL Corp.
$25 billion
Dec. 2002

FACTOID

The world's smallest snake is as thin as pencil lead.

COLOSSAL ARENA

The Colosseum is an amphitheater in Rome, Italy. When it was finished, just under 2,000 years ago, it could hold 50,000 spectators. The Colosseum—which means "giant place"—was used for gladiator battles in which slaves fought each other to the death. The Colosseum's arena was normally filled with sand, but it could also be flooded so gladiators could fight using boats.

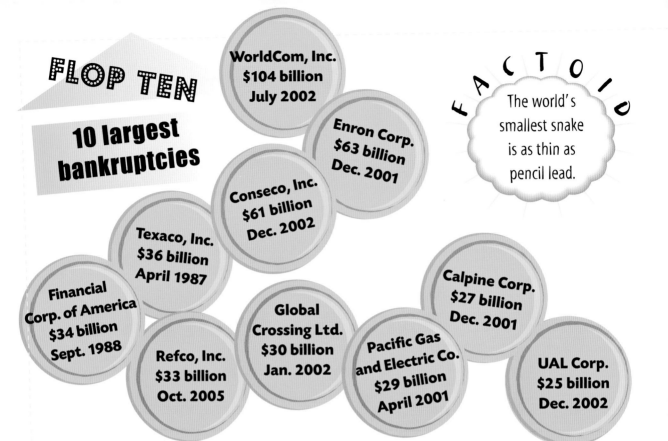

Zorbing is a fun activity in which people roll down a hill strapped inside a giant padded ball. The Zorb was invented in New Zealand in the 1980s. Zorbonauts, as the riders are called, are now found across the world, from China to Norway and Argentina. A popular alternative is the hydrozorb. It contains water that flows around the sphere as it rolls, carrying the rider with it.

KUIPER BELT

The Kuiper (pronounced "kyper") belt is a ring of icy blocks that orbit the sun at the edge of the solar system. The Kuiper belt contains many millions of objects that are like dirty snowballs—a mixture of rock and ice. These objects are left over from the formation of the planets. Most astronomers now think that Pluto, once thought to be the smallest and most distant planet, is actually a large member of the Kuiper belt.

clones

W–O–R–M–H–O–L–E

Check out:
Dolly
Page 54

Organisms that have exactly the same genes as each other.

Nerd Word

SEE

The most printed book is the Bible. More than 4 billion copies have been printed—and 24 million new ones are added each year.

The oldest known printed book is the Diamond Sutra. This religious Chinese book was made in A.D. 868.

SAW

LA TOMATINA

La Tomatina is a giant tomato fight that takes place each August in Buñol, a small town near Valencia, Spain. Several thousand people gather in the town square to take part. The event begins with a competition to unhook a large ham from the top of a greased pole. Then more than 100 tons (91 tonnes) of rotten tomatoes are delivered to the square on trucks. The organizers fire a cannon to start the fight—and the mayhem begins!

TSUNAMI

FACTFILE

Tsunamis are giant waves that are created by an earthquake or landslide at the bottom of the sea.

The word tsunami means "harbor wave" in Japanese. It is not possible to see the wave out at sea, it only rises up high in shallow water near the land.

A tsunami travels at up to 500 miles per hour (800 km/h) through deep water. As it nears land, it slows down and rises up to 100 feet (30 m) above sea level.

In 2004, a tsunami in the Indian Ocean killed nearly 200,000 people in 12 countries, from Indonesia to Africa.

SEE SAW

The world's newest country is Montenegro. This became a separate country in 2006 after it seceded from Serbia.

The oldest country in the world is Iran. It has been independent since 539 B.C. For most of this time it was known as Persia.

FACTOID

The name Wendy was first used in the book *Peter Pan*.

50

Tour the TOWER

The Eiffel Tower is the most famous building in Paris, France. The French know it as *La Tour Eiffel*. It is named after its designer, Gustave Eiffel, who built the tower for the 100-year celebrations of the French Revolution in 1889. The tower is made from iron. It is 985 feet (300 m) tall, which made it the tallest building in the world until 1930. It still has a great view of Paris, and more than 5 million visitors ride to the top every year.

GOOF-A-THON

Nonstick Pans

Some pans are coated in a wax called Teflon. Teflon is superslick, so no food gets stuck on the bottom of the pan. That makes it much easier to clean. Teflon was discovered by accident. In 1938, Roy Plunkett, an American chemist, found that a flask of gas had become a slippery solid. The solid was polytetrafluoroethylene, so it was renamed Teflon for short. Teflon is also used in waterproof coats and is woven into space suits.

Who built the first car?

Page 32

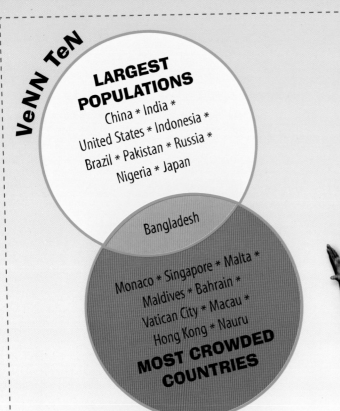

LARGEST POPULATIONS

China * India *
United States * Indonesia *
Brazil * Pakistan * Russia *
Nigeria * Japan

Bangladesh

Monaco * Singapore * Malta *
Maldives * Bahrain *
Vatican City * Macau *
Hong Kong * Nauru

MOST CROWDED COUNTRIES

First BUNGEE JUMP

The first modern bungee jump was made on April Fools' Day in 1979. Four members of the Dangerous Sports Club tied long elastic ropes to the Clifton Suspension Bridge in Bristol, England. They then jumped off, much to the horror of passersby. However, the jumpers were perfectly safe. Today, hundreds of thousands of people make bungee jumps every year.

Drinking BLOOD

Vampire bats drink blood. Their usual victims are cattle and chickens, but they also attack people. Just like Count Dracula, the bats have long fangs, which they use to prick a hole in their victim's skin. The bats then lick up the trickle of blood. Chemicals in the bat's spit stop the cut from forming a scab.

SUPER SENSES

SHARKS: They can sense the electricity produced by the muscles of other animals. Their electrosensors are sensitive enough to detect an animal's heart beating.

SALMON: Adult salmon swim back to the river in which they were born. They can pick up the smell of their home rivers from far out at sea.

DOLPHINS: These sea mammals use a fatty "melon" on the tops of their heads to focus beams of high-pitched sound. The echoes from the sound beam help the dolphin find food. These beams might also be used to stun prey.

INSECTS: Many insects, such as butterflies, taste with their feet, so they know if they want to eat something just by walking on it.

JUMPING SPIDERS: A jumping spider is a tiny hunter. It uses a total of eight eyes for tracking prey. The two largest eyes are bigger than the spider's brain.

FORMULA 1 FLAGS

During a Formula 1 race, officials communicate with the drivers using colored flags.

RACE FINISHED

RACE STOPPED

DANGER, SLOW DOWN

DRIVER MUST LEAVE CIRCUIT

TRACK SLIPPERY

NONRACING CAR ON THE TRACK

MOVE OVER TO LET FASTER CAR OVERTAKE

DANGER ON TRACK HAS BEEN REMOVED

GRANITE

Granite is a common type of rock made up of three minerals: feldspar, quartz, and mica. Granite is made when hot liquid rock, called magma, rises to just below the surface of the earth. The magma slowly cools to form granite. Granite is usually found in single huge lumps—some are hundreds of miles wide.

Dolly THE Sheep

Dolly the sheep was the first cloned mammal. She was born in 1996. Dolly had no father. All of her DNA came from a female sheep. This was put into the womb of another sheep, where it grew into a lamb. Dolly died in 2003, much sooner than a normal sheep, of a lung disease that is common in old sheep. Some scientists think that she died younger because she was a clone.

FACTOID

The world's narrowest street is St. John's Lane in Rome. It is 19 inches (48 cm) wide.

World's SMELLIEST fruit

A durian is a large, spiky fruit that grows in Southeast Asia. It is about the size of a soccer ball and is filled with flesh that tastes like custard, a type of milk-based pudding. However, the fruit is better known for its awful smell, which is a cross between rotting fish and a dirty toilet. The fruit is popular, but not with everyone. As a result, it is banned from hotels and trains.

GOOF-A-THON

Discovering America

Christopher Columbus is the most famous explorer in the world. There is even a country named after him. However, Columbus stumbled upon North America by accident. He was trying to reach the Indian Ocean and thought it would be quicker to sail west. (The eastern route was a long journey around Africa.) Columbus was not the first European to reach North America. The Vikings arrived there 500 years before he did.

ROCKS FROM SPACE

The flash of a shooting star is not caused by a star at all, but a small piece of space rock. The solar system is full of these rocks, known as meteoroids. When one hits the atmosphere, it gets very hot and burns up in a flash. That is what we see as the shooting star, or meteor. If a meteor is large, it will not all burn up in the air. The pieces that hit the ground are called meteorites. They often contain a lot of rare metals.

PeOPLe-OPOLY

Annie Edson
(1838–1921)

Annie Edson was the first person to survive a ride over the Niagara Falls in a barrel. Annie wanted to become famous. In 1901, she came up with the barrel-ride idea and padded the inside of a pickle barrel with a mattress. Air was then pumped inside before the barrel was set adrift in the Niagara River. The current pulled the barrel to the Horseshoe Falls. Annie cut her head but was otherwise unhurt.

Stat-O-Sphere

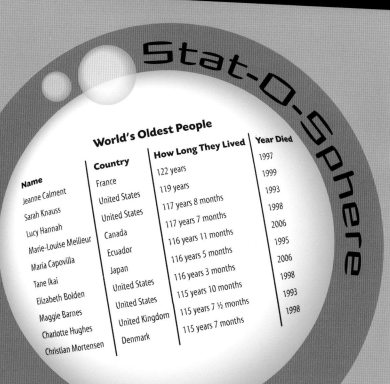

World's Oldest People

Name	Country	How Long They Lived	Year Died
Jeanne Calment	France	122 years	1997
Sarah Knauss	United States	119 years	1999
Lucy Hannah	United States	117 years 8 months	1993
Marie-Louise Meilleur	Canada	117 years 7 months	1998
María Capovilla	Ecuador	116 years 11 months	2006
Tane Ikai	Japan	116 years 5 months	1995
Elizabeth Bolden	United States	116 years 3 months	2006
Maggie Barnes	United States	115 years 10 months	1998
Charlotte Hughes	United Kingdom	115 years 7 ½ months	1993
Christian Mortensen	Denmark	115 years 7 months	1998

WORLD'S LEAST POLLUTED COUNTRIES

Finland * Norway * Canada * Switzerland * New Zealand * Australia * Austria * Iceland * Denmark

Sweden

United States * France * Japan * Germany * Russia * South Korea * United Kingdom * Canada * Ukraine

LARGEST USERS OF NUCLEAR POWER

GO FOR A SPIN

Have you ever heard the phrase, "like a whirling dervish"? People use it to describe someone who is rushing around very busily. However, a real whirling dervish is a dancer from the Turkish city of Konya. The religious dance involves spinning around for hours while chanting to music.

Ancient Egyptian women used dark blue eye makeup that contained radioactive uranium.

TUSK FACE

The babirusa is one of the weirdest looking pigs in the world. Its name means "pig deer," and if you ever see one, you'll understand why—it has two curved spikes growing out of its face! They are too low down to be antlers but too high up for tusks. In fact, they are two of the animal's top teeth, but instead of growing down, they grow upward—through its skin. The lower teeth form tusks, too. Female babirusas have much smaller tusks than the males.

SHINE ON

A harvest moon occurs when a full moon rises at about the same time as when the sun is setting. So although the sun has set, the night never really gets very dark because of the light from the moon. This phenomenon is known as a harvest moon because it occurs in fall, when farmers are harvesting crops. This is a busy time, and thanks to the harvest moon, farmers can see well enough to work all night.

Check out:
Moon Walk
Page 45

TINT hints

Chemicals called pigments are responsible for hair color. Eumelanin is a dark pigment, while pheomelanin is red. Black hair has mostly eumelanin in it. Brown hair has a lot of both pigments, but less eumelanin makes hair blonde. Hair that has just phaeomelanin has red coloring. Hair turns gray when the body stops making pigments.

CLIFF CASCADE

A long white cliff at Pamukkale, southern Turkey, is known as Cotton Castle by the local people. From across the valley, the cliff sparkles in the sunlight. Up close, the cliff is a series of limestone pools that form a steplike cascade down the hill. The pools are formed by the minerals left behind by spring water. The ancient Greeks built a city above the cascade.

DRUM KIT!

Crash cymbal

Ride cymbal

Hi-hat cymbal

Tom-tom

Snare drum

Drum kits, or drum sets, have a number of different drums and cymbals that can be played by a single performer.

Tripod

Bass drum

WANTED

Dick Turpin
(1705–1739)

Also known as: Richard Turpin
Birthplace: Essex, England
Crimes: Stealing cattle, poaching, and highway robbery

Dick Turpin is remembered as a dashing villain who robbed wealthy travelers before escaping on his beautiful horse, Black Bess. Turpin's life of crime started when he was a butcher's boy and stole cattle from local farms. In 1735, Dick became a highwayman—an armed bandit who attacked travelers on empty roads. The police eventually caught him and Turpin was hanged in 1739.

REWARD

placebo

A medicine that cures an illness because someone believes it will.

Nerd Word

TYPES OF KNOTS

reef knot **two half hitches**

clove hitch **square knot**

overhand knot **slipknot**

BLOOD GROUPS

There are four main blood groups: A, B, AB, and O.

Each blood group has a certain chemical coating the blood cells.

Healthy people donate a little of their blood so it can be given to someone who is severely hurt.

A person's blood group tells doctors what type of blood an injured person can receive.

O blood can be given to anyone. AB blood can only be given to people in the AB blood group.

FACTPILE

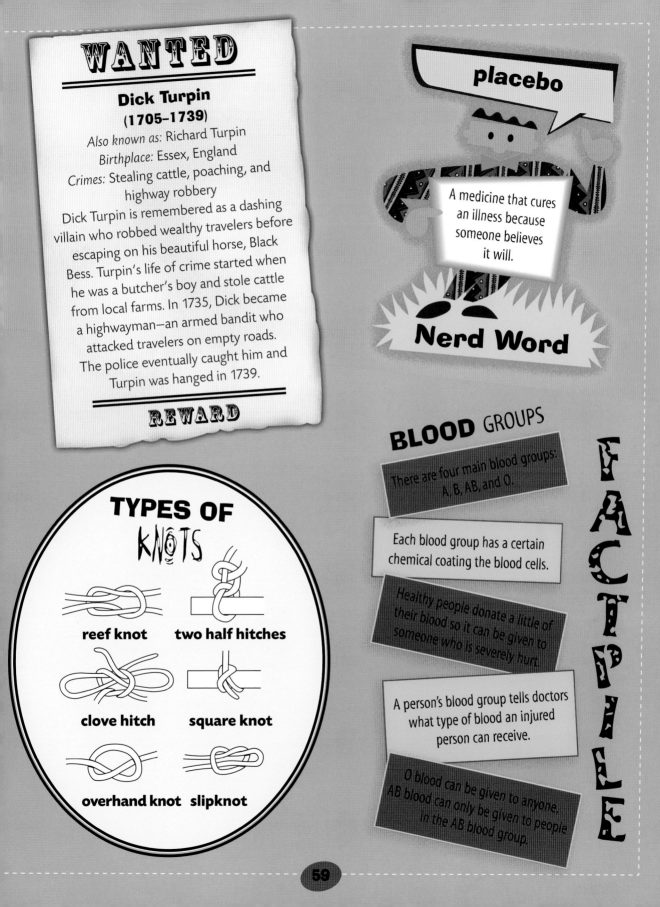

FACTFILE

ROCKETS

A rocket is powered by burning fuel that is directed through a small hole, or nozzle.

Rocket fuel does not need air to burn, so it can work in space.

The first rockets were fireworks made in China in the tenth century.

The largest rocket ever used was the *Saturn V*. It could carry the weight of 12 trucks into orbit.

The BLUE Men

The Tuareg people live in northwest Africa. Many now live in cities, but some still live a traditional life as nomads. They have no permanent home and travel around on camels. Tuaregs are sometimes called the Blue Men because their headdresses are made from blue cloth. Tuaregs once guided huge caravans, or trading parties, across the Sahara.

RED IN THE FACE

The red uakari is a monkey that lives in the flooded forests of western South America. It is sometimes called the English monkey because it reminds local people of a sunburned tourist.

In what year was the laser invented?

GOOF-A-THON

Cornflakes

In the 1870s, two brothers, W. K. and John Kellogg, set up a health farm, where people stayed to become healthy. The Kellogs served them a homemade mixture of wheat and fruit. Many years later, the Kellogs left some boiled wheat in an unsealed container by mistake. They tried to roll it into a sheet, like pastry, but discovered that the grains produced flakes. Once toasted, these flakes became the world's first cornflakes.

DARK Glass

Obsidian is natural glass. It is made when lava cools down very quickly, such as when it flows into water. Obsidian is very dark and hard. Before people had discovered how to make metal objects, many ancient civilizations used obsidian to make shiny mirrors and sharp tools.

The decathlon is an athletics competition for men. Decathlon competitors have to be all-around athletes because they take part in ten events: high jump; long jump; pole vault; shot put; javelin; discus; 110-meter hurdles; and 100-meter, 400-meter, and 1,500-meter runs. They win points for each event and the man with the most points wins. Women compete in heptathlons, which have seven events.

100 m.

400 m.

1,500 m.

BIOMES

The world's land is divided into several types of landscapes called biomes. Areas within each biome share a similar climate and, as a result, they have the same types of wildlife. The more common biomes include deserts and mountains. There are also rain forest, marine, tundra (the coldest one), and even cave biomes.

Desert

Tundra

Rain forest

What is the world's largest **invertebrate?**

Page **18**

PeOPLe-OPOLY

Estevanico
(1503–1539)

Estevanico was the first African-American. He was the Moroccan slave of a Spanish explorer. In 1528, he was shipwrecked on what is now the coast of Texas. After eight years exploring the area, Estevanico reached the Spanish colony of Mexico. He had heard stories about cities made of gold and was asked to lead a search for them. He traveled ahead of his companions, but when he arrived at the first Native American town, the chief had him chopped into pieces.

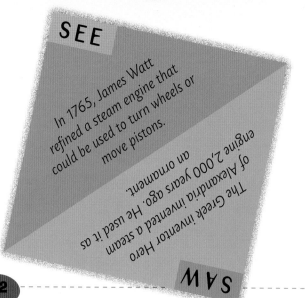

SEE

In 1765, James Watt refined a steam engine that could be used to turn wheels or move pistons.

The Greek inventor Hero of Alexandria invented a steam engine 2,000 years ago. He used it as an ornament.

SAW

A light-year is a unit used to measure the huge distances between stars. A light-year is the distance light travels in a year. A beam of light travels 186,410 miles (300,000 km) in just one second. In a year, it travels 5.9 trillion miles (9.5 trillion km). Astronomers think the Universe is at least 28 billion light-years across!

AROUND the BEND

VeNN TeN

LARGEST ISLANDS

New Guinea * Borneo * Madagascar * Baffin Island * Sumatra * Great Britain * Honshu * Victoria Island * Ellesmere Island

Greenland

Canada * Indonesia * Russia * Philippines * Japan * Australia * Norway * United States * New Zealand

COUNTRIES WITH LONGEST COASTLINES

The Guggenheim Museum in Bilbao, Spain, is one of the weirdest buildings in the world. Its curved walls are covered in metal and glass. The architects used computers to figure out how to make a building with so many bends.

MAD ABOUT FLOWERS

Tulips are bell-shaped flowers that grow wild in Asia. They were first grown in Europe about 500 years ago. Tulips quickly became popular and growers could not produce enough. The price of tulip bulbs became high, and wealthy families gave bulbs as wedding gifts! By the 1630s, tulips were often grown in gardens across Europe and prices dropped.

W-O-R-M-H-O-L-E

Check out:
Stinking Flower
Page 43

TYPES OF HATS

Boater

Trilby

Bowler (Derby)

Panama

Fez

Astrakhan

Mortarboard

Deerstalker

THORNY Devil

The thorny devil is a spiky-looking lizard that lives in the deserts of Australia. The spikes defend it against predators, but they also have another purpose. There is no water in the desert, so the lizard must drink in another way. In the morning and evening, tiny droplets of dew form on the lizard's back. Its spikes provide a large surface area for the dew, which then trickles to the lizard's mouth through tiny channels between the scales.

FACTFILE

RINGS OF **SATURN**

Saturn's rings are made up of lumps of rock and ice mixed with dust.

The rings are thousands of miles across but only 330 feet (100 m) thick.

The rings are either the remains of a shattered moon or the leftovers from when the planet formed.

Giant rocks, called shepherd moons, orbit around the edge of the rings.

A Collection of Collective Nouns

A parliament of owls
A host of angels
A herd of horses
A poverty of pipers
A wealth of information
A team of oxen
A run of salmon
A stand of trees

WANTED

Genghis Khan
(c.1162–1227)

Also known as: Temujin
Birthplace: Mongolia
Crimes: Wild and brutal murderer

Genghis Khan was probably not as bad as people believe. He was the first ruler of the Mongol Empire—the largest empire the world has ever known. He built a huge army of fierce horsemen, which he used to conquer most of China and Central Asia. After Genghis's death, Mongol armies continued to expand the empire and raided Eastern Europe. Over the years, Genghis Khan became linked to the dangers of the Mongol hordes.

REWARD

Genes

The code that contains the instructions for making a living body.

Nerd Word

A FEATHER

Bird feathers are made from keratin, the same stuff in hair and fingernails. The feathers' barbs, or strands, are hooked together to make a single flat surface.

Vane

Rachis

Shaft

Barb

After-feather

TWISTED TREE

Stat-O-Sphere

World's biggest selling songs

Title	Artist (year released)	Numbers sold (as singles)
Candle in the Wind	Elton John (1997)	37 million
White Christmas	Bing Crosby (1942)	30 million
Rock Around the Clock	Bill Haley and His Comets (1954)	17 million
I Want to Hold Your Hand	The Beatles (1963)	12 million
Hey Jude	The Beatles (1968)	10 million
It's Now or Never	Elvis Presley (1960)	10 million
I Will Always Love You	Whitney Houston (1992)	10 million
Hound Dog	Elvis Presley (1957)	9 million
Diana	Paul Anka (1957)	9 million
I'm a Believer	The Monkees (1966)	8 million
(Everything I Do) I Do It For You	Bryan Adams (1991)	8 million

maelstrom

A powerful, even violent, whirlpool that can suck up objects nearby.

Nerd Word

Box jellies are deadly sea creatures that live in the waters around New Guinea and northern Australia. The jellyfish are named after their cube-shaped bodies. Their tentacles are packed with harpoon-shaped stingers that fire on touch. A box jelly sting can kill a person. Most of the people who die are children.

Strangler figs are unusual plants because they begin life at the top of a tree. A monkey leaves a sticky seed on a high branch after eating a fig. The fig's roots grow down the tree trunk and into the ground. Meanwhile, the fig's branches spread through the top of the tree, using it as a platform to reach the sunshine. Over many years, the fig's leaves swamp the tree, and its roots completely surround the trunk. Eventually, the tree inside is strangled to death, and the fig roots form a hollow twisted tower. It is now a race against time for the fig to spread seeds to the neighboring trees before the plant comes crashing down.

SADDLE

There are two common types of saddles for riding a horse: the Western saddle (below) and English saddle. The choice depends on your riding style.

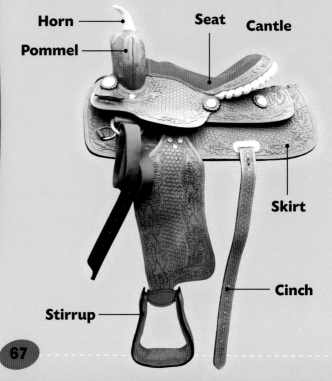

Horn

Pommel

Seat

Cantle

Skirt

Cinch

Stirrup

WAT A SIGHT!

Wat Pho is a large Buddhist temple in Bangkok, Thailand. The temple has more than 1,000 images of the Buddha, including the largest one in the world: the Reclining Budda. This statue is 480 feet (146 m) long—almost the size of an Olympic swimming pool. It is 50 feet (15 m) high. Apart from the soles of the giant feet, every inch of the statue is covered in gold plate.

FACTOID

Budgerigar is an Australian Aboriginal word for "good food."

Helpless Queen

Termites are insects that live in giant families called colonies. They live inside mounds of mud. All the members of a colony have the same mother and father. They are the king and queen and live at the heart of the nest. The queen spends all of her time laying eggs. She swells up and cannot do anything for herself. Her children feed her, keep her clean, and care for her eggs.

PeOPLe-OPOLY

Tim Berners-Lee
(1955–)

Every day, millions of people look at Web sites to buy things, chat, and find information. They all use a computer program called a Web browser, which lets them search and view Web pages. The Englishman Tim Berners-Lee created the first Web browser in 1990, and in doing so, he invented the World Wide Web. Tim also came up with Web terms such as html, http, and url.

W-O-R-M-H-O-L-E

Check out:
Ada Lovelace
Page 57

SEE

Today's largest North American city is Mexico City, 30 miles (50 km) south of Teotihuacán. Mexico City is home to 22 million people.

Before European settlers arrived in America, Teotihuacán, in what is now Mexico, was the largest city, with 250,000 inhabitants.

SAW

VeNN TeN

LARGEST ARMIES IN WORLD WAR I

Germany * Great Britain * France * Austria-Hungary * Italy * Turkey * Bulgaria * Japan

United States * Russia

India * China * North Korea * South Korea * Pakistan * Iran * Turkey * Egypt

LARGEST ARMIES IN 2007

Who Kept the DOGS OUT?

The world's longest fence is in Australia. The wire barrier stretches 3,300 miles (5,310 km) from coast to coast. It was built in the 1880s to stop wild dogs, or dingoes, from entering the area to attack sheep. It also kept the dingoes from hunting kangaroos on the south side of the fence, so there are now too many kangaroos.

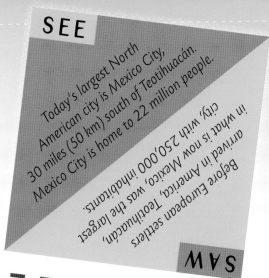

FLOATING ON AIR

The fastest trains are maglev trains. They have top speeds of about 250 miles (402 km) per hour. Maglev stands for "magnetic levitation." Magnets attract each other, but they also push apart. A maglev train and its track have powerful magnets that push the train along using that force. When it goes fast enough, the train floats in the air.

SUNSPOTS

Sunspots are dark areas on the surface of the sun.

At just 5,430°F (3,000 °C), a sunspot is half the temperature of the rest of the surface.

The spots are caused by tangles in the sun's magnetic field.

Sunspots occur in a 22-year cycle. According to some scientists, when there are few sunspots, the earth's weather is colder.

W—O—R—M—H—O—L—E

Check out: the Sun Page 17

WANTED

Fletcher Christian
(1764–1793)

Birthplace: Cockermouth, England
Crimes: Mutineer

Fletcher Christian was the captain's mate aboard HMS *Bounty*. In 1789, Christian led a mutiny, or uprising, and took command of the ship from the captain, William Bligh. Bligh was set adrift in a small boat and was lucky to make it to dry land. Christian and the other mutineers settled down on the remote island of Pitcairn.

REWARD

TERRIBLY BEAUTIFUL

With so many colorful, bulb-shaped domes and intricate wall carvings, St. Basil's Cathedral is Russia's most memorable building. And it was built to be just that. The first czar, or king, of Russia, Ivan the Terrible, built the cathedral after a great victory in war during the 1550s. Legend has it that Ivan had the church's designer blinded so he could never make a more magnificent building.

When was the first **cloned mammal** born?

Page 54

INTERCESSION CATHEDRAL (ST. BASIL'S)

All **EYES**

Tarsiers are tiny relatives of monkeys and lemurs that live in the forests of Southeast Asia. They hunt at night for insects and little frogs and have huge eyes to find their way in the dark. A tarsier's eyes are enormous compared to its body, and are larger than the animal's brain. Such huge eyes can't swivel, so the tarsier twists its head from side to side to scan the forest.

HOLI SMOKE!

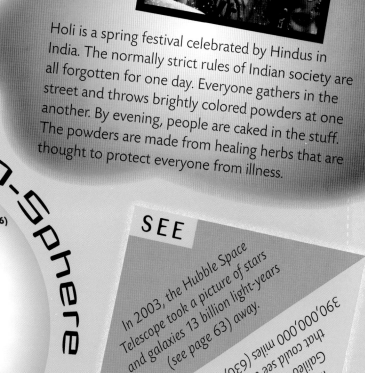

Holi is a spring festival celebrated by Hindus in India. The normally strict rules of Indian society are all forgotten for one day. Everyone gathers in the street and throws brightly colored powders at one another. By evening, people are caked in the stuff. The powders are made from healing herbs that are thought to protect everyone from illness.

Stat-O-Sphere

World's busiest airports

Name	Location	Number of passengers (2006)
Hartsfield–Jackson	Atlanta, Georgia	84,846,639
O'Hare	Chicago, Illinois	77,028,134
Heathrow	London, England	67,530,197
Haneda	Tokyo, Japan	65,810,672
Los Angeles	Los Angeles, California	61,041,066
Dallas–Fort Worth	Dallas, Texas	60,226,138
Charles de Gaulle	Paris, France	56,849,567
Frankfurt	Frankfurt am Main, Germany	52,510,683
Beijing Capital	Beijing, China	48,654,770
Denver	Denver, Colorado	47,325,016

SEE

In 2003, the Hubble Space Telescope took a picture of stars and galaxies 13 billion light-years (see page 63) away.

In 1610, the Italian scientist Galileo Galilei built a telescope that could see the moons of Jupiter 390,000,000 miles (630,000,000 km) away.

SAW

FLOP TEN

Shortest-serving leaders

1. Luís Filipe
King of Portugal for less than 30 minutes on February 1, 1908

2. Roger LaFontant
President of Haiti for four hours on January 7, 1991

3. Joseph Goebbels
Chancellor of Germany for five hours between April 30–May 1, 1945

4. Boris Yeltsin
Prime Minister of Russia (as well as President) for six hours on March 23, 1998

5. Carlos Manuel Piedra
President of Cuba for 12 hours on January 2, 1959

6. Siaka Stevens
Prime Minister of Sierra Leone for less than 24 hours in March 1967

7. Skënder Gjinushi
President of Albania for one day in July 1997

8. Ratu Tevita Momoedonu
Prime Minister of Fiji for one and a half days in March 2001

9. Diosdado Cabello
President of Venezuela for two days in April 2002

10. Dipendra
King of Nepal for three days (despite being brain-dead) in June 2001

How long is the largest canyon?

Page **42**

FACTOID
In Iran, seven items starting with the letter S are set on a table as a New Year tradition.

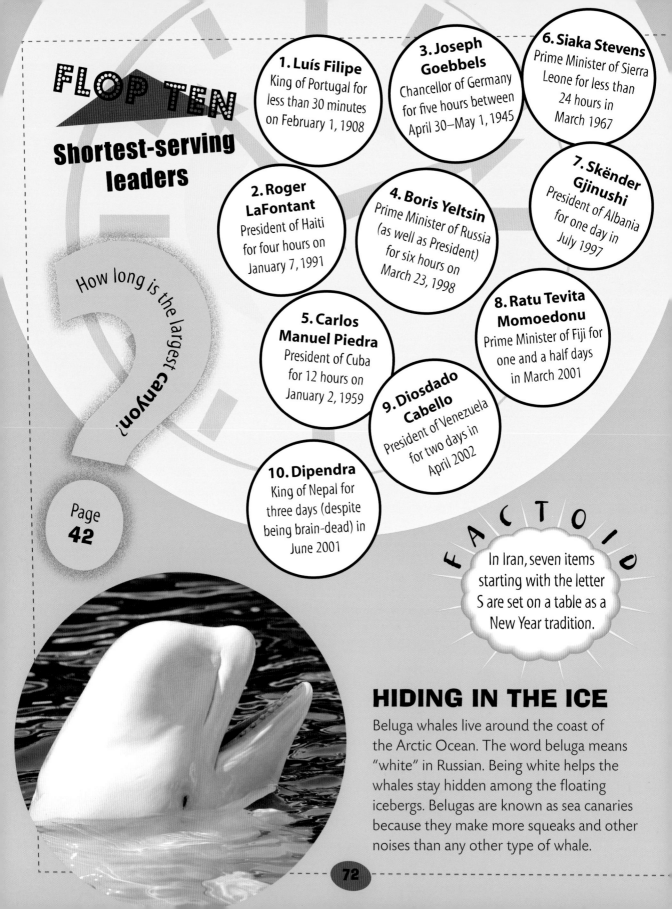

HIDING IN THE ICE

Beluga whales live around the coast of the Arctic Ocean. The word beluga means "white" in Russian. Being white helps the whales stay hidden among the floating icebergs. Belugas are known as sea canaries because they make more squeaks and other noises than any other type of whale.

Welcome to the
MINI-SEA OF SIBERIA

Lake Baikal in Siberia is the largest lake in the world. No other lake contains so much water. With 330 rivers flowing into it, one-fifth of all fresh water on the earth is held by Lake Baikal. The lake is 395 miles (636 km) long and about 1 mile (1.6 km) deep, making it the deepest hole on land. Lake Baikal is a mini-sea—it even has its own species of seal!

NUMERALS

Western	Arabic	Roman	Siamese
0			
1		I	
2		II	
3		III	
4		IV	
5		V	
6		VI	
7		VII	
8		VIII	
9		IX	

BRASS INSTRUMENTS

Trombone

Trumpet

Tuba

French horn

IN A SPIN

In the northern hemisphere, water goes down a drain in a counterclockwise direction. In the southern hemisphere, it goes down the other way. This is also true of the direction in which hurricane winds spin. This effect is due to the Coriolis force, which is caused by the rotation of the earth. For example, when a wind blows north from Florida to New York, the surface of the world, with the land, spins away to the east. So the wind never reaches New York but instead curves around across North America.

VeNN TeN

SUNNIEST PLACES

Yuma, Arizona * Phoenix, Arizona * Bordj Omar Driss, Algeria * Bilma, Niger * Keetmanshoop, Namibia * Aoulef, Algeria * Upington, South Africa * Atbara, Sudan * Mariental, Namibia

Wadi Haifa, Sudan

Arica, Chile * Asyut, Egypt * Dakhla Oasis, Egypt * Al Kufrah, Libya * Bender Qaasim, Somalia * Iquique, Chile * Dongola, Sudan * Faya-Largeau, Chad * Masirah Island, Oman

DRIEST PLACES

Hidden Jewels

A geode is a bubble inside a rock that forms when the rock is cooling down. The hollow part of the geode often contains a layer of colorful crystals. The largest geode yet found was 26 feet (8 m) wide.

Aqueduct

A bridge that carries a channel of water across a valley.

Nerd Word

Macaw

Lovebirds

Cockatoo

Lorikeet

Parrots

DUSTUP

In the 1930s, the prairies of North America were hit by a drought—it hardly rained for several years in a row. The farmers in certain areas, such as Oklahoma and Kansas, had to let the soil in their fields dry out and turn to dust. This dust was whipped up by the winds into huge storms that turned the sky black and covered everything in dirt. For several years, the land became a "dust bowl" where nothing could be grown.

PeOPLe-OPOLY

Samuel Morse
(1791–1872)

In the 1830s, Samuel Morse developed a device, known as a telegraph, to send messages down wires. Although telegraphs have not been used for several decades, the communication system invented by Morse—the Morse code—is still sometimes used. The code of dots and dashes (short and long tones) can be sent by taps, flashes of light, and beeps. The SOS signal in Morse code is simple—dot dot dot; dash dash dash; dot dot dot.

Between Two Oceans The Panama Canal is a waterway that cuts across a narrow strip of land called the Isthmus of Panama. At the western end, ships enter from the Pacific Ocean. The eastern end of the canal joins the Atlantic. The canal allows ships to move between these oceans, without having to travel all the way around South America.

Where is the most **active volcano**?

Page
37

A HOUSE Fit for a GOD

There are 106 temples in India that, Hindus believe, are the homes of Lord Vishnu. Hindus try to visit every one before they die. The largest and most magnificent of these temples is Sri Ranganathaswamy Temple in Tamil Nadu in southern India. This immense complex is surrounded by seven sets of walls. After passing 29 towers, worshippers arrive at the Hall of 1,000 Pillars (which has only 953 pillars). Although the temple has been in use for at least 2,000 years, it was only finished in 1987.

W–O–R–M–H–O–L–E

Check out:
Holi
Page 71

One Light, MANY Colors

White is not really a color. Instead, it is light that contains a mixture of every color. If white light is split up, a rainbow of colors is produced. Isaac Newton, a great physicist, named this set of colors the spectrum. The spectrum begins with red and ends with purple, and it is impossible to count how many other colors are in between. However, Newton divided the spectrum into seven colors—red, orange, yellow, green, blue, indigo, violet—because he thought seven was a magic number.

An ETERNAL Youth

The axolotl is a salamander that lives in two lakes in central Mexico. The Aztecs believed that the axolotl was the ugly brother of the splendid dragon god Quetzalcoatl. They gave it its name, which means "monster." Most salamanders spend the early part of their lives under water. Then they replace their gills with lungs and come out onto the land. However, the axolotl never makes this change.

GREAT and SMALL

The world's largest monkey is the mandrill of Africa. It lives in the forest, but at 44 pounds (20 kg), it is too heavy to climb very high into the trees.

The world's smallest monkey is the pygmy marmoset of Peru and Ecuador. This monkey is 200 times smaller than the mandrill and is light enough to climb on large blades of grass.

200 X !

Stat-O-Sphere

Top 10 heaviest birds		
Name	Weight lb. (kg)	Can it fly?
Ostrich	344 (156)	No
Cassowary	128 (58)	No
Emu	121 (55)	No
Emperor penguin	101 (46)	No
Greater rhea	55 (25)	No
Mute swan	50 (22.5)	Yes
Kori bustard	42 (19)	Yes
Andean condor	33 (15)	Yes
Great white pelican	33 (15)	Yes
Egyptian vulture	28 (12.5)	Yes

EAST or WEST

Experts think that Polynesians—the people who live in Hawaii and the other islands in the Pacific—originally came from Asia. But Norwegian Thor Heyerdahl thought that they had come from South America. To prove this was possible, he built a wooden raft called *Kon Tiki* in 1947 and set sail from Peru. It arrived at the islands of Polynesia 100 days and 4,275 miles (6,880 km) later.

SWEET ANTS

Honeypot ants have an odd way of storing food. Some of the ants in the colony are stuffed with food by other workers. These ants convert the huge meals into a sweet liquid, similar to honey. The ants swell up to a huge size. They hang from the roof of the nest, while the rest of the colony sips honey from them.

Sparkling STONE

Marble is a hard and shiny stone that is used to make fine buildings and sculptures. The best marble is white, but some marbles are mixed with colored minerals. Marble starts off as flaky limestone, but it is heated and squeezed deep inside a mountain so that it turns into a hard stone.

Castle

In the Middle Ages, whoever owned a castle in Europe ruled the surrounding area. But castles became useless 400 years ago when cannons that could smash the stone walls were developed.

Tower

Inner wall

Outer wall

Outer gate

SKY CITY What is the oldest town in the United States? The answer might surprise you. It is not New York or Boston but a collection of mud-brick houses in New Mexico. People have been living in Acoma, a Native American pueblo, or village, for at least 900 years. The village is known as Sky City because it is built on top of a mesa—a steep-sided hill with a flat top. There is only one way up or down.

STINGING NETTLE

FACTFILE

The stinging nettle is a plant found in many parts of the world.

The plant is named for its ability to sting. Nettle is from the Saxon word for "needle."

Nettle stings are caused when hairs on the leaves poke into the skin. The hairs are coated with acid.

Squeezing a nettle leaf firmly flattens most of the hairs so you don't get stung as much. The phrase "grasp the nettle" means "be brave and it won't be so bad."

SEE

In 1959, Hawaii became the 50th state in the United States of America.

The United States of America became a nation in 1776, when it was made up of 13 states.

SAW

FACTOID

Cadillacs are named after the French explorer who founded Detroit, where the cars are made.

Ice from the Sky

Hailstones form when raindrops are blown upward by winds. The water is carried so high that it freezes. The balls of ice become too heavy and fall as hail. Most hailstones are a fraction of an inch across. However, if winds are strong, they can be 6 inches (15 cm) wide!

FROZEN in Time

Many trees leak a sticky substance called resin. It works a little like a scab to fill in gaps in the bark. Dollops of resin sometimes fall to the ground. If conditions are right, after a few million years, the resin becomes amber. Amber is normally orange. People make it into jewelry. Scientists also look to see what tiny animals, such as mosquitoes, have been trapped inside.

ARMORED Anteater

The giant armadillo grows to about 5 feet (1.5 m) long. It lives in the forests of South America, surviving on ants. It digs into the ants' nest with long claws before licking the insects up with its sticky tongue. The armadillo holds its breath when it digs so it doesn't suck in any dust. Once inside, it will slurp up tens of thousands of ants in a single meal.

CLIMBING A WATERFALL

The Montmorency Falls pour into the St. Lawrence River a little way downstream from Quebec, Canada. The falls are about 100 feet (30 m) taller than Niagara Falls, but every winter they freeze solid. Ice climbers come from across the world to scale the frozen slope.

FLOP TEN
April Fools

1. Swiss Spaghetti Harvest (1957): A British television news program announced a good spaghetti harvest, thanks to great weather—but, of course, spaghetti isn't a plant that is grown.

2. Sidd Finch (1985): A U.S. sports magazine told the story of new star pitcher Sidd Finch, who had learned to throw a baseball by meditating in Tibet.

3. Nylon Color TV (1962): The chief engineer of Sweden's only television station showed viewers how to convert their black-and-white pictures to color by putting a nylon stocking over the screen.

4. Taco Liberty Bell (1996): The U.S. fast-food chain Taco Bell announced that it had bought the Liberty Bell—the bell struck when the United States became independent.

5. San Serriffe Islands (1977): A British newspaper published a travel article about pretend islands that were shaped like punctuation marks.

6. Nixon's Third Term (1992): An American radio station announced that the disgraced ex-president Richard Nixon was running for president again.

7. New Pi (1998): A science journal reported that the Alabama government had decided to alter the value of pi to 3.0.

8. Eating Left-Handed (1998): Burger King published an ad announcing new hamburgers designed to be eaten by left-handed people.

9. Ice Borers (1995): An American science magazine reported that Dr. Aprile Pazzo had discovered an animal living in the Antarctic—a hotheaded ice borer!

10. Gravity Reduced (1976): A famous British astronomer announced on the radio that at 9:47 A.M. on April 1, gravity would be so low, people would float inside their houses.

SOFT WOOD

Corks are made from the inner bark of an oak tree that grows in Spain and the surrounding area. The bark is full of air pockets, which makes the wood soft. It can be squeezed to fit into bottles. However, the cork is airtight—air and water cannot pass through it.

Four EGYPTIAN Gods

Ra: The sun god and creator, he had the head of a hawk. Egyptians believed that Ra took the form of a scarab beetle, which rolls balls of dung. Ra rolled the sun across the sky each day.

Isis: The mother goddess of Egypt, Isis became a goddess after tricking Ra into being bitten by a snake.

Anubis: As the god of the dead, Anubis had the head of a jackal.

Thoth: The god of wisdom, he had the head of a bird.

W-O-R-M-H-O-L-E

Check out:
Mummy
Page 39

TOOTHY MONSTER

ASPIRIN

Aspirin was first made from the bark of a willow tree. It cures mild pain, such as headaches, and reduces fevers. Some people with heart problems take aspirin because it helps blood move around the body.

Gharials are strange-looking crocodiles that live in India and Nepal. They have very long, narrow snouts lined with more than 100 sharp teeth. A gharial slashes its mouth through the water to catch fish, which are swallowed whole. Male gharials have a knob, or pot, on the tip of their snouts. These are used to blow bubbles and make loud buzzing noises to attract females.

SHAKA DAY

Every September thousands of Zulu men and women gather in KwaDukuza, in South Africa. That is where the great Zulu leader, King Shaka, died in 1828. Many wear traditional clothes made from the skins of calves and leopards. The men perform war dances and hold a tournament, using short clubs called knobkerries. The women have dancing competitions.

FACTFILE

Stromatolites

Stromatolites are the oldest living things on the earth. Some are 3.5 billion years old.

Each stromatolite is made up of millions of ultrathin layers of minerals. The minerals are the remains of ancient bacteria.

The bacteria grow on top of the remains of the last layer, slowly adding to the stromatolite.

Some stromatolites are still alive. The best place to see them is Shark Bay, Australia.

TALLEST TREES

The world's tallest living tree is a coast redwood that grows in California. It is 378 feet (115 m) high and must be more than 1,000 years old. However, the tallest tree ever recorded was a 469-foot (143-m) eucalyptus tree in Australia. It was measured in 1885 but has now died.

MOVING up the MOUNTAIN

Abu Simbel is a temple built by Ramses II beside the Nile River in Egypt more than 3,000 years ago. In the 1960s, the temple was cut into 16,000 blocks and moved to higher ground, so it wouldn't be covered by water when a dam was built on the river.

W-O-R-M-H-O-L-E

Check out:
Sphinx
Page 9

VeNN TeN

TOP FISH-EATING COUNTRIES

Maldives * Iceland * Kiribati * Japan * Seychelles * Portugal * Malaysia * French Polynesia * South Korea

Norway

Saudi Arabia * United States * Russia * Iran * Mexico * Venezuela * China * United Kingdom * Iraq

BIGGEST OIL-PRODUCING COUNTRIES

PeOPLe-OPOLY

Joseph Marie Jacquard
(1752–1834)

Frenchman Joseph Marie Jacquard invented an automatic loom, or weaving machine. French weavers were outraged because the machine did most of their work for them, and they got paid a lot less. In many factories, the workers smashed it using their wooden clogs, called sabots. The defiant workers became known as saboteurs.

DROOPY Nose

You won't forget seeing a saiga. This weird animal from Central Asia has a long, floppy nose that hangs over its mouth. Nobody is quite sure what a saiga is. Scientists think it is a link between antelopes and wild goats. It is suggested that the big nose is used as a filter to stop dust from getting into the lungs. During the mating season, the males' noses swell up and their faces get covered in sticky gunk.

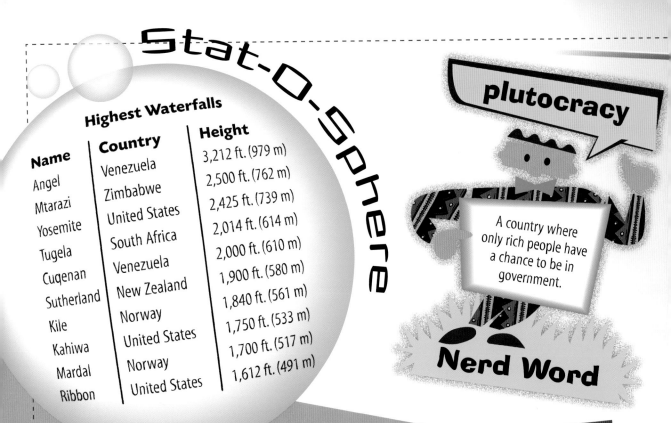

Stat-O-Sphere

Highest Waterfalls

Name	Country	Height
Angel	Venezuela	3,212 ft. (979 m)
Mtarazi	Zimbabwe	2,500 ft. (762 m)
Yosemite	United States	2,425 ft. (739 m)
Tugela	South Africa	2,014 ft. (614 m)
Cuqenan	Venezuela	2,000 ft. (610 m)
Sutherland	New Zealand	1,900 ft. (580 m)
Kile	Norway	1,840 ft. (561 m)
Kahiwa	United States	1,750 ft. (533 m)
Mardal	Norway	1,700 ft. (517 m)
Ribbon	United States	1,612 ft. (491 m)

plutocracy

A country where only rich people have a chance to be in government.

Nerd Word

PeOPLe-OPOLY

4th Earl of Sandwich
(1718–1792)

The most famous Earl of Sandwich was John Montagu, a English politician and naval commander in the 18th century. The earl worked long hours in his office and often missed dinner. That was an easy thing to do because dinner was served at four o'clock in the afternoon! The earl decided to eat while working at his desk. He ate salt beef between two pieces of toast—and invented the sandwich!

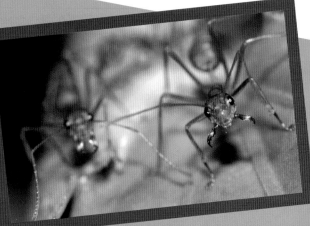

THE FAMILY HOME

Weaver ants build their nest of leaves. Dozens of ants fold leaves over so their edges touch, while other workers begin the sticking process. For this, the ant larvae—little maggotlike babies—make a sticky silk, which is used to stitch the leaves into a small box for the queen ant and her eggs. When the nest is too crowded, some of the ants move out and make a new one.

SPINNING WINGS

What do you get if you cross a plane with a helicopter? The answer is a gyroplane, which was invented in the 1920s. A gyroplane has the body of a small plane with a propeller engine that provides the power. However, instead of wings, the flying machine has a rotor—two or three rotating blades. The rotor just spins around as air rushes over it. That spin is enough to lift the gyroplane off the ground.

GIGA WHAT?

In the metric system, "centi-" is added to "meter" to make centimeter, a one-hundreth of a meter. Adding "kilo-" makes kilometer, one thousand meters. But have you ever wondered what a nanosecond is? Or a megaton, terawatt, and gigabyte? This table will help you out. The system works in the same way, but add a different word to show a bigger number or tinier fraction.

1,000,000,000,000 One trillion **TERA-**
1,000,000,000 One billion **GIGA-**
1,000,000 One million **MEGA-**
1,000 One thousand **KILO-**

CENTI- One hundredth 0.01
MILLI- One thousandth 0.001
MICRO- One millionth 0.000001
NANO- One billionth 0.000000001

NEUTRON STAR

A neutron star is a small dark object in space. It may be small—about 12½ miles (20 km) across—but it contains more material than is in our sun! One teaspoon of neutron star weighs a billion tons. Neutron stars are made when giant stars explode and then fall in on themselves.

GETTING COLD FEET

The emperor penguin is the only animal to spend the winter on Antarctica. They survive temperatures of -40°F (-40°C) for weeks at a time. How come they don't freeze to the ground? The answer lies in the birds' feet. Each blood vessel carrying warm blood into a foot is surrounded by a vessel carrying cold blood out of the foot. The warm blood cools down and the cold blood heats up, and that makes the penguin's feet chilly. Cold feet won't melt the ice, so they won't refreeze to the ground in the polar conditions.

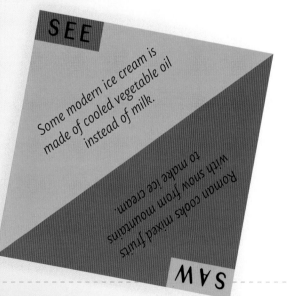

SEE

Some modern ice cream is made of cooled vegetable oil instead of milk.

SAW

Roman cooks mixed fruits with snow from mountains to make ice cream.

SLANG words

judder bar: speed hump (New Zealand)
snag: sausage (Australia)
guagua: bus (Cuba)
lekker!: nice! (South Africa)
gorby: tourist (Canada)
scratcher: bed (Ireland)
wilwil: bicycle (Papau New Guinea)
go-slow: traffic jam (Nigeria)

OPEN SEASON

In February, thousands of fishermen gather at Argungu, on the Sokoto River in Nigeria. They travel there for the annual fishing competition. The competitors have an hour to catch the largest fish. Most fishermen work in pairs. One carries a net, while the other keeps them afloat with a hollow gourd. The winner takes home one million niara ($8,000).

THREE ELEMENTS

Elements are nature's building blocks. They are combined in different ways to make certain substances. Here are three very different elements:

 HYDROGEN: The lightest element of all, hydrogen is a colorless gas. Hydrogen is found in water, sugar, oil, acids, and plastic. Stars contain mainly hydrogen.

FE IRON: A common type of hard metal, iron is mixed with other things to make steel. It is also found in blood.

 SULFUR: One of the nonmetal elements, sulfur is a bright yellow powder. Sulfur is used by living things. Also bad, eggy smells contain sulfur.

WHALE of a Time

Hermanus, a few miles east of the Cape of Good Hope in South Africa, is one of the best places in the world to see whales. Gray whales go to the town's bay to give birth. When one arrives, the town's Whale Crier blows his horn to let everyone know to go to the cliffs and watch. In August, Hermanus holds a birthday party for all the whale calves born that year.

MINARET

FACTFILE

A minaret is a tower on a mosque, the place where Muslims go to worship.

Traditionally, Muslims are called to pray at the mosque from a balcony at the top of a minaret.

The only mosque to have seven minarets is the Ka'aba, Islam's holiest site in Mecca.

The muezzin is the person who sings the call to prayer from the minaret.

W–O–R–M–H–O–L–E

Check out:
The Dome
Page 94

LINES in the SEA

Early sailors had a problem. Once they were out of sight of land, they couldn't be sure where their ship was or how to get to where they wanted to go. Latitude is a system that helps pinpoint a position on the earth. A place's latitude is given as a number of degrees (°) from the equator. The equator is the line that goes around the middle of the globe. Its latitude is 0°. The North Pole has a latitude of 90° north. The latitutude of Tampa, Florida, is 27° north. Until modern times, sailors would have to measure the height of the sun at noon to figure out their latitudes.

FACTOID

Neanderthals had larger brains than modern humans.

pragmatism

To do whatever is needed to get results, even if it means changing a plan.

Nerd Word

Catching a CABLE

San Francisco's famous streetcars have no engines. Instead, they are pulled by a cable that runs under the street. A mechanism called a grip extends out of the bottom of the streetcar and through a slit in the road, where it holds on to the cable. Onboard, the grip man releases the car from the cable when it is time to stop, then reattaches the grip to start again.

Largest Moons in Solar System

Name	Planet	Diameter
Ganymede	Jupiter	3,270 miles (5,262 km)
Titan	Saturn	3,201 miles (5,151 km)
Callisto	Jupiter	2,996 miles (4,821 km)
Io	Jupiter	2,274 miles (3,660 km)
The Moon	Earth	2,159 miles (3,475 km)
Europa	Jupiter	1,939 miles (3,121 km)
Triton	Neptune	1,682 miles (2,707 km)
Titania	Uranus	980 miles (1,577 km)
Rhea	Saturn	950 miles (1,529 km)
Oberon	Uranus	946 miles (1,522 km)

Which dog is the smallest dog in the world?

Page **35**

GOOF-A-THON

Say Cheese!

Cheese was probably invented more than 5,000 years ago in Central Asia. The traditional way of carrying liquid in Central Asia is in a pouch made from a goat's stomach. Putting milk into a pouch that was not dried out would turn the milk into a lumpy mush—the first cheese. Chemicals in the stomach lining turned the millk into cheese. Today, we still make cheeses by mixing the same chemicals into tanks of milk.

Capybara

The people of South America also call capybaras water hogs. However, capybaras are actually giant versions of guinea pigs, and they are more closely related to a mouse than to a pig you might see on a farm. Capybaras eat the grass that grows on riverbanks. They live in large groups for saftey, and when a jaguar or a giant snake comes in for the kill, the whole herd sprints into the water with a splash to get away.

Countries with the MOST NURSES

San Marino * Ireland * Norway *
Finland * Netherlands * Iceland *
UK * Switzerland * Denmark

Belarus

Estonia * Ukraine * Russia *
Latvia * Lithuania * Armenia *
Hungary * Georgia * Monaco

Countries with MORE WOMEN than men

REMOTE STATUES

Easter Island is one of the most remote pieces of land on the earth. The island, which is part of Chile, is also known for being the home to more than 600 giant statues. Many of them are buried in the ground so only their heads are showing. The largest is as tall as a house. No one is sure, but the statues were probably built after important people died. Building big things has continued on Easter Island. It also has a huge runway built by NASA as an emergency landing strip for the space shuttle.

SKYLAB

In the early 1970s, NASA, the U.S. space agency, had planned many missions to the moon. However, when the Russians put a space station into orbit, NASA realized that was more important. They quickly built their own space station. The result was Skylab, which was launched in 1973. Skylab stayed in orbit until 1979.

Hindenburg DISASTER

The *Hindenburg* was the largest passenger airship ever built. It was 800 feet (244 m) long—as long as a cruise ship—and had a top speed of 60 mph (97 km/h). The German airship was built to fly people across the Atlantic Ocean to the United States and Brazil. The *Hindenburg* was filled with hydrogen, a light but highly explosive gas. Disaster struck in 1936 when the airship was about to land in New Jersey. A spark set a gas leak alight and the airship was engulfed in fire. Of the 96 people onboard, 36 died and most of the others were injured.

Water Monster

A hellbender is a real-life water monster. This giant salamander from the swamps and pools of the eastern United States grows to 2 feet (60 cm) long. A hellbender is a hunter and it catches crayfish, fish, and insects in ambushes using a powerful suck. When a victim is near, the monster opens its wide mouth. Water rushes into it, which drags the prey in, too.

Dome of the Rock

A large golden dome in Jerusalem, Israel, is one of the holiest places for Muslims. The dome houses a rock at the top of a hill. Muslims believe that the prophet Muhammad flew to heaven from that rock to meet God, who gave him the knowledge to start the religion of Islam.

Wedding **Ducks**

In Korea, a bride and groom are presented with a pair of carved wooden ducks by their families. Traditionally, the groom's mother throws one of the ducks to the bride, who catches it in her skirt. If the bride catches the duck, her first baby will be a boy. If she drops it, she will have a daughter.

Blue morpho

When it is sitting with its wings folded, the blue morpho looks like a dull butterfly. However, when it flutters through the forest, flashes of shimmering blue can be seen on the tips of the wings. This vibrant color is produced by light bouncing off different layers of the surface.

Types of TEETH

Most adults have 32 teeth. There are four main types, which are found in equal numbers on both sides of the mouth:

1. INCISORS: There are eight of these teeth at the front of the mouth. They are for biting off pieces of food.

2. CANINES: These four fang-shaped teeth are also called eye teeth because the top ones are positioned under each eye.

3. PREMOLARS: A total of eight premolars are found at the sides of the mouth. Unlike incisors and canines, premolars have two points each, used for cutting and grinding food.

4. MOLARS: The back 12 teeth are called molars. They are the largest teeth in a person's mouth. They are wide and bumpy for crushing food. The last four molar teeth are called wisdom teeth because they do not grow until a person is fully grown-up. Some people never grow wisdom teeth.

FLOP TEN

The cost of clearing up the world's disasters over the last 15 years.

1. Winds and storms: $499 billion
2. Floods: $353 billion
3. Earthquakes: $306 billion
4. Droughts: $64 billion
5. High temperatures: $63 billion
6. Forest fires: $35 billion
7. Factory accidents: $28 billion
8. Tsunamis: $8 billion
9. Avalanches and landslides: $5 billion
10. Volcanoes: $4 billion

RUBY Red

Rubies are a precious type of stone that sparkle with a deep red color. Because they are hard, they are a good stone to use in jewelry. Rubies are made from a mineral called corundum. It usually has crystals that are transparent, or can be seen through. When a tiny piece of chromium is mixed in, the crystal becomes ruby red.

WANTED

Mata Hari
(1876–1917)

Birthplace: Leeuwarden, Netherlands
Crimes: Spy

During World War I, Mata Hari was a beautiful nightclub dancer in Paris. She had many soliders as boyfriends, who told her many military secrets. She was accused of passing these secrets to the enemy German army. It is not clear if Mata Hari was a spy, but she was still shot by a firing squad in 1917.

REWARD

FACTOID

Sperm whales have the largest brains of any animal. At more than 15 pounds (7 kg), they are five times bigger than a human's.

Rich Men

In 1981, the computer company IBM needed a program, called an operating system, that would make the parts of a personal computer work together. They knew that Gary Kildall, a programmer, had such a system, but he decided to go flying instead of meeting with them. So IBM went to Bill Gates at Microsoft. His deal with IBM helped to make him one of the richest men in the world.

The largest hunter on land is the Kodiak bear, a type of grizzly that lives on the islands of southern Alaska. A Kodiak bear is as big as a family car. A single blow from the bear's paw is enough to smash a person's skull. Despite its great strength, a Kodiak bear spends most of its time looking for fruits and nuts.

Two GIANTS

The largest hunting animal of all is the sperm whale. This mighty creature grows to 62 feet (19 m) long and has 28 teeth the length of a man's hand. Sperm whales eat giant squids, wrestling with them 3,280 feet (1 km) below the surface.

Swimming to Asia

The Hellespont is a channel of water in Turkey that joins the Black Sea to the Mediterranean. The western bank is in Europe, and Asia is on the eastern side. Every year swimmers from around the world race across it from Europe to Asia. The journey is about 3 miles (5 km) and is swum in 2 hours.

Joseph Kittinger
(1928–)

Joseph Kittinger has fallen farther than anyone else on the earth. In 1960, he was part of an American project to test if humans could survive in space. Kittinger flew to the edge of space in a balloon wearing an early space suit. He went to 102,700 feet (31,303 m), the highest anyone has ever been in a balloon. Kittinger could not land his balloon, so he parachuted. He jumped into space and fell for 4½ minutes. On the way down he reached 714 mph (1,149 km/h), the fastest anyone has fallen. The space suit worked, and Kittinger landed safely.

POWER SURGE

Every 12 hours, the gravity of the moon pulls seawater up beaches and rivers. This is high tide. Six hours later, the same effect pulls the water in the other direction out to sea, making low tide. Tidal power stations use this flow of the water into and out of rivers to spin special propellers called turbines. The spinning turbines generate electricity. Because tides are powered by the moon, they will never run out.

Stat-O-Sphere

Longest Caves

Name	Place	Length
Mammoth Cave	United States	367 miles (591 km)
Jewel Cave	United States	135 miles (218 km)
Optimisticeskaja	Ukraine	133 miles (215 km)
Wind Cave	United States	123 miles (198 km)
Hollöch	Switzerland	120½ miles (194 km)
Lechuguilla Cave	United States	120 miles (193 km)
Fisher Ridge	United States	110 miles (177 km)
Sac Actun	Mexico	96 miles (155 km)
Siebenhengste-hohgant	Switzerland	95½ miles (154 km)
Ox Bel Ha	Mexico	91 miles (147 km)

Who created a code of dots and dashes?

Page
75

Set in STONE

Great Zimbabwe, which means "stone houses," is the ruins of an ancient African city in southern Zimbabwe. Experts think that about 200,000 people lived there 800 years ago. It was the center of a civilization that controlled land all the way to the Indian Ocean. Traders from Arabia and India arrived to buy gold. By the 15th century, Great Zimbabwe appears to have been abandoned. Nobody knows why.

HOLD Your Breath

Kabaddi is a game played in India and Bangladesh. Two teams of seven players line up on opposte sides of a court. Each team takes turns to send a raider into the opposition half. This raider must hold his breath while in enemy territory. He shouts "kabaddi, kabaddi" over and over to prove he is not breathing. The raider tries to tag a defending team member so he will be sent off. The defending team must stay in a chain as it tries to surround the raider so he cannot return to his half. The game continues until all the players of one team have been sent off.

FACTOID

If the sun went out, it would take eight minutes before people on the earth noticed.

F-SCALE

The strength of tornadoes, or whirlwinds, are measured using the F-scale, devised by Japanese-American Ted Fujita.

F0: Light
40–72 mph (64–116 km/h)
Chimneys damaged; branches broken; small trees pushed over.

F1: Moderate
73–112 mph (117–181 km/h)
Roofs damaged; mobile homes overturned; cars pushed off the road.

F2: Considerable
113–157 mph (182–253 km/h)
Roofs torn off; mobile homes demolished; large trees snapped.

F3: Severe
158–206 mph (254–332 km/h)
Walls torn off houses; trains overturned; most trees uprooted; cars lifted off the ground.

F4: Devastating
207–260 mph (333–418 km/h)
Strong houses leveled; weak houses blown some distance.

F5: Incredible
261–318 mph (420–512 km/h)
Strong houses lifted off foundations and carried along; car-size objects flung through the air farther than 330 feet (100 m); bark ripped off trees.

SEE

The Pan-American Highway is today's longest road. It runs 47,720 miles (76,800 km), from Alaska to southern Argentina.

The Royal Road of the Persian Empire in the 5th century B.C. ran 1,677 miles (2,699 km), from present-day Turkey to Iran.

SAW

FLAT HEADS

The Chinooks are Native American people who lived near the mouth of the Columbia River in Washington state. Having a flat, sloping forehead was a sign of beauty to a Chinook. Their babies were transported in papooses, or flat cradles. The babies were strapped in for safety, and a wooden board was kept pressed gently on their foreheads. This forced the baby skulls to grow with flat foreheads. Flattened skulls have been found all over South America, showing that it was not only the Chinooks who did this.

A jewel beetle can smell wood smoke from 50 miles (80 km) away.

pulsar

A spinning star that sends out pulses, or beams, of radiation.

Nerd Word

BLACK GOLD

Crude oil, or petroleum, is valuable stuff. It is a mixture of chemicals that can be used to make everything from fuel for cars and airplanes to plastic foam, soap, and aspirin. The chemicals in oil are made from the remains of living things that were buried tens of millions of years ago. The mix of chemicals is divided out into sections called fractions. The light fraction contains flammable liquids, such as diesel. The medium fraction contains thick oil and soft material, such as wax. The heavy fraction is sticky sludge, such as tar.

The FLIP SHIP

One of the most unusual ships ever made is FLIP. FLIP is an ocean research vessel based in San Diego. It has no engine, so it is towed everywhere. Its name stands for Floating Instrument Platform. When it is in deep water, FLIP actually does a flip, too. Water is pumped into one end of the vessel so that part sinks under the water. The other end is lifted up into the air. Living onboard FLIP is complicated. Each bathroom has two toilets, one on the floor, the other on a wall, and rooms have at least one door in the floor or ceiling.

Lines in the Sand

No one knows why the ancient people of Nazca created large shapes in the deserts of Peru 2,000 years ago. The 70 shapes of animals and plants were created by grooves cut into the dark ground, exposing paler rock underneath. These shapes are so large they can only be seen from high in the sky. The shapes were rediscovered in the 1920s, when pilots saw them from planes. Some people suggest the lines were made for aliens visiting in spacecraft. Others think the Nazca people had hot-air balloons!

DOWNHILL all the way!

Helmet protects the head during falls.

The suit is tight so it does not create drag.

Poles help the skier to keep balance during turns.

The skis are long and the top ends are wider, so they travel over the top of the snow quickly.

Ski boots are stiff, so the skier and skis move as a single unit.

Longest Journey

Kangaroos, koalas, and possums are a type of animal called a marsupial. A marsupial mother does not have room to grow babies inside her body, so marsupial joeys, or babies, are born when they are small. They have no back legs and look like a pink worm with two claws on their front legs. The joeys use the claws to drag themselves to their mother's pouch. Once in the warm pouch, the joeys continue to grow.

VeNN TeN

TOP FORESTED COUNTRIES (BY PERCENTAGE)
French Guiana * Solomon Islands * Surinam * Gabon * Guyana * Brunei * Belau * North Korea

Finland * Sweden

China * United States * India * Brazil * Indonesia * Canada * Russia * Nigeria

TOP TIMBER-PRODUCING COUNTRIES

Sea of Weeds

A large part of the western Atlantic Ocean is known as the Sargasso Sea. The sea is named after the huge amounts of sargassum there. Sargassum is a floating seaweed that gathers in the area because of the calm water. Large currents move around the edges of the Sargasso Sea, but that leaves a section of deep, calm water in the middle. Christopher Columbus sailed through the Sargasso Sea on his first voyage to the Americas in 1492.

NOT SO CHARMING

For centuries, snake charmers have wowed crowds by controlling deadly cobra snakes with their eerie hypnotic music. However, it is all an act. The charmer keeps his snake in a basket. The snake is happy coiled up in the dark. When the charmer takes the lid off the basket, the snake is not so happy. It rises up to scare away any attackers. It would do that if the charmer played or not.

What causes a giant **tsunami**?

Page **50**

Stat-O-Sphere

Most successful Olympic athletes

Athlete	Country	Event	Number of medals
Larissa Latynina	USSR	Gymnastics	18 (9 gold)
Nikolay Andrianov	USSR	Gymnastics	15 (7 gold)
Boris Shakhlin	USSR	Gymnastics	13 (7 gold)
Edoardo Mangiarotti	Italy	Fencing	13 (6 gold)
Takashi Ono	Japan	Gymnastics	13 (5 gold)
Paavo Nurmi	Finland	Track and field	12 (9 gold)
Kato Sawao	Japan	Gymnastics	12 (8 gold)
Mark Spitz	United Sates	Swimming	11 (9 gold)
Matt Biondi	United States	Swimming	11 (8 gold)
Vera Cáslavská	Czechoslovakia	Gymnastics	11 (7 gold)

Marco POLO

In 1271, at the age of 17, Marco Polo left his home in Venice and traveled through Asia to China.

Polo went with his father and uncle, who were merchants. They were among the first Europeans to visit eastern Asia.

The Polos spent 17 years living with the court of Kublai Khan.

Marco Polo sailed most of the way home and wrote about his adventures.

Olympus Mons

The largest mountain in the solar system is not on Earth. It is not even on Jupiter, but on Mars, one of the smallest planets. At 16¾ miles (27 km) high, Olympus Mons is three times as tall as Mount Everest.

FACTOID

The world's longest-lasting lightbulb has been used in a fire station in California for 106 years.

Rats Meet Ants

Naked mole rats live in burrows under the deserts of southern Africa. They never come above the surface. The rats live in a family group arranged like a colony of ants or termites. Only the leading female in the family has babies. The smell of her pee stops others from trying to take over. The smaller, younger rats dig the tunnels and find most of the food. The large male rats sit at the edge of the burrow to fight off snakes or other hunters.

Land of Extremes

Antarctica is the coldest, windiest, and driest continent on the earth. The lowest temperature ever recorded, -128.56°F (-89.2°C), occurred there. The air over Antarctica gets so cold that it plummets to ground level as a powerful wind that rarely drops below 30 mph (48 km/h). Blizzards are common. There is a lot of water in Antarctica, but it is all solid ice. There is less liquid water there than you'd find in the world's driest deserts.

Staying WET in the DRY

Frogs like it wet, and that includes one species that lives in billabongs in northern Australia. A billabong is a water pool that fills up with rainwater. In droughts, a billabong might dry out completely. An ordinary frog would die, but the water-holding frog knows what to do. It burrows into the deep mud as the billabong dries out. Then its outer layer of skin becomes loose and forms a bag around the frog. The bag is filled with slime, which keeps the frog damp, even when it is bone-dry on the surface.

Greatest Show on the Earth

The Carnival in Rio de Janeiro, Brazil, is the largest party on the earth. The carnival is a celebration of Mardi Gras, a feast day that marks the start of the buildup to Easter. The party is centered on a parade through Copacabana, the city's beachside district. People in extravagant costumes dance through the streets to samba music. Competitors from Rio's many samba schools compete in dancing competitions that are bigger than soccer matches. During Carnival, the already crowded city swells with tens of thousands of tourists and everyone has a good time!

Dam big

The largest chunk of concrete in the world is China's Three Gorges Dam, on the Yangtze River. The dam is about 1¼ miles (2 km) wide and almost as tall as the Golden Gate Bridge. Behind the dam is a lake about 373 miles (600 km) long. Ships sail along it from the ocean to the city of Chongqing.

vacuum

A space that has nothing in it, not even air.

Nerd Word

Author: Tom Jackson
Managing Editor: Ellen Dupont
Cover Design: Becky Terhune
Designer: Leah Germann
Editor: Theresa Bebbington
Picture Researcher: Amy Smith
Proofreader: Marion Dent
Indexer: Michael Dent

ISBN-13: 978-0-545-05333-4
ISBN-10: 0-545-05333-1

10 9 8 7 6 5 4 3 2 1   08 09 10 11 12

First printing, November 2008

Picture Credits